# SKI SNACKS

# SKI SNACKS

## EASY, TASTY RECIPES FOR POWDER DAYS AND MOUNTAIN ADVENTURES

Lily Krass Ritter and Max Ritter

SKIPSTONE

**Dedicated to our families: Erika and Gerd,
John and Cynthia, and Henry**

Copyright © 2025 by Lily Krass Ritter and Max Ritter
All rights reserved. No part of this book may be reproduced or utilized in any form, or by any electronic, mechanical, or other means, without the prior written permission of the publisher.

Published by Skipstone, an imprint of Mountaineers Books—an independent, nonprofit publisher. Skipstone and its colophon are registered trademarks of The Mountaineers organization.
Printed in China
28 27 25 25          1 2 3 4 5

Design: Ellis Failor-Rich
All photos by the authors unless otherwise indicated.
Frontispiece: *A very hungry skier drops into a classic Teton line*

Library of Congress Cataloging-in-Publication data is on file for this title at https://lccn.loc.gov/2025932414

Printed on FSC®-certified materials.

ISBN (paperback): 978-1-68051-787-3
ISBN (ebook): 978-1-68051-788-0

Skipstone books may be purchased for corporate, educational, or other promotional sales, and our authors are available for a wide range of events. For information on special discounts or booking an author, contact our customer service at 800.553.4453 or mbooks@mountaineersbooks.org.

Skipstone
1001 SW Klickitat Way
Suite 201
Seattle, Washington 98134
206.223.6303
www.skipstonebooks.org
www.mountaineersbooks.org

**LIVE LIFE. MAKE RIPPLES.**

# CONTENTS

**TWO HUNGRY SKIERS**  *9*
    Ski Snacking Is All about Trial and Error  *16*

**MAKING YOUR OWN SNACKS**  *25*
    Stocking the Pantry  *29*
    Tools and Equipment  *34*
    How to Package Your Own Snacks  *40*
    What Kind of Ski Snacker Are You?  *44*
    Don't Bonk: Tips for Staying Fueled  *46*

**HOW TO USE THIS BOOK**  *49*
    Recipe Ratings  *51*
    Cooking at Altitude  *54*

**SAUCES AND SPREADS**  *57*
    Aioli, Three Ways  *59*
    Everyday Pesto  *61*
    Sundried Tomato and Olive Tapenade  *62*
    Miso Peanut Sauce  *65*
    Quick Plum Rhubarb Jam  *67*
    Homemade Nutella  *68*

**QUICK BITES**  *71*
    Energy Balls, Five Ways  *72*
    Bacon and Date Rice Bars  *76*
    Cheesy Polenta Bars  *78*
    Oatmeal Banana Cookies, Three Ways  *80*
    Jammy Banana Thumbprints  *82*
    Ants on a Date  *84*

Pocket Quiche, Two Ways   *86*
Bacon-Wrapped Dates with Goat Cheese   *89*
Chocolate-Dipped Pocket Bacon   *90*
Crispy Nut Butter Bars   *92*
Mads Balls   *94*
Apple-Brie Prosciutto Roll-Ups   *97*
Onigiri, Three Ways   *98*
SPAM Musubi   *103*
Quick Candied Spiced Nuts, Four Ways   *105*
Schnitzel Strips   *108*

## SUMMIT SANDWICHES   *111*

Pesto, Egg, and Avocado   *112*
Tomato Jam and Arugula Breakfast Sammie   *114*
Le Chamoniard Baguette   *117*
Smashed Chickpea and Avocado   *120*
Powder Day Turkey Club   *123*
Grilled Halloumi and Harissa   *124*
Classic Caprese   *126*
Turkey, Apple, Brie, and Honey   *129*
The Tram Waffle   *130*
Skid Luxury French Toast PB&J   *132*
Kimchi Grilled Cheese   *134*
Pocket Dillas, Four Ways   *138*
The Brooklyn Italian   *141*

## BAKED GOODS   *143*

Lemon Yogurt Cake   *144*
Fudgy Espresso Brownies   *146*
Trail Mix Chocolate Chip Cookies   *150*
Cinnamon Roll Flatbread   *152*
Bribery Banana Bread   *154*
Handheld Apfelstrudel   *157*

Mini Orange Marzipan Cakes   *160*
Chocolate Chairlift Cookies   *162*
Scallion and Cheese Waffles   *164*
Backcountry Biscuits   *166*
Butter Mochi Cake   *168*

## SIPPABLES   *171*

Miso Honey-Lemon Water   *173*
Soul-Warming Carrot Ginger Soup   *174*
Mudslide Mocha   *177*
Dirty Honey Chai Tea   *179*
Miso Ramen Broth   *181*
Iced Earl Grey Maple Tea   *183*
The Italian   *185*
Chunky Monkey Smoothie   *187*
The Spaghett or the Skid Spritz   *189*
The Older but Not Grown-Up Old Fashioned   *190*
The Corpse Reviver   *191*
Salted Maple Iced Coffee   *192*
Salted Maple Lemonade   *193*

## TAILGATE TREATS   *195*

Chocolate-Blueberry Recovery Smoothie   *196*
Berry Chia Yogurt Parfait   *199*
Charcuterie Board   *203*
Tailgate Pizza, Three Ways   *205*
The Skid Pizza   *207*
Bail Cake   *208*
Eat Pasta, Ski Fasta   *210*

*Acknowledgments*   *213*
*Recipes by Rating*   *214*
*Index*   *216*

# TWO HUNGRY SKIERS

On a cold, crisp morning in the mountains of Colorado, eighteen hungry college kids were crammed like sardines into a six-person backcountry ski yurt. The two of us met while flipping pancakes—scooping batter into an oversized cast iron skillet, replenishing the lumpy pre-ski sustenance from a family-sized bag of pancake mix.

We were skiing on Cameron Pass for the weekend with the University of Colorado Boulder's Backcountry Ski Club, an all-inclusive weekend trip that cost just twenty dollars a head—gas, lodging, and food were subsidized thanks to some clever footwork from our club president. We routinely packed two dozen skiers into small spaces—hallways and kitchen floors were perfectly acceptable places to roll out a sleeping bag on a college ski trip—and ate our weight in PB&Js, pancakes, and bulk breakfast sausage to keep costs down. We skied all day long before collapsing into a heap inside an overstuffed yurt or rental house, stuffing our faces, and washing everything down with PBR (which probably made up half the budget).

Fortunately, pancake mix didn't remain a recurring part of our relationship, but feeding friends and family, either for a ski day or impromptu dinner party, most certainly did. When we moved to the Tetons to start a life together in the mountains, food and skiing would become inextricably intertwined.

We both grew up in families that prioritized food, whether that was gathering around the table each night for a home-cooked meal or dreaming up creative dishes to enjoy while camping. Lily was raised thirty minutes outside of Seattle, enjoying the bounty of the area's produce by way of a weekly CSA from a local Snoqualmie Valley farm. Although she was raised on home-cooked meals, it wasn't until moving away to college that she began learning to cook for herself. Max, on the other hand, grew up in the hustle and bustle of New York City, with absolutely zero shortage of international cuisines to explore. While eating his way through the city

*Opposite: Enjoying an alpine spring outing in Wyoming's Teton Range*

was a daily routine, he too was raised on home-cooked meals inspired by his parents' time growing up in Germany, living in Italy, and appreciating the value of food from one's own kitchen.

In Jackson, Wyoming, we fell head over heels in love with everything about mountain-town life—the midweek powder mornings, backyard barbecues, running into friends in the tram line. We both had ideas of what life as a skier in a mountain town might look like, both imagining we'd live this life for a year or two, "get it out of our system," and see where the winds blew us next. But it didn't take long to discover that there's more to mountain living than the activities that initially drew us in. It wasn't the proximity to the mountains that kept us in Jackson; it was the people we met, people who wove us into the fabric of the community, who made us want to stay.

Jackson is where we were first introduced to the term "skid," a Teton term for ski bum. We can't take credit for the term, but we did write our own definition, which we hope whoever coined it will find accurate:

**Skid [noun]:** *A certain individual commonly found in mountain towns all over the world who prioritizes "getting after it" above real responsibilities. Expert in finding happy-hour deals, not paying for their own lift ticket, and consuming a diet consisting largely of ramen, pizza, smooshed PB&Js, and discount lagers.*

*Used in a sentence: "Look at that skid over there stealing french fries from a six-year-old in ski school."*

The only part of the ski-bum lifestyle that we couldn't get on board with was the diet. There's a classic stereotype of a ski bum stirring ketchup into a paper cup of hot water and calling it "soup." That was never the true reality of modern-day ski bummery, but it was easy to slip into a routine of greasy pizza between lift laps, free granola bars, smushed PB&Js, and candy on the skintrack.

One day, after a long ski tour in Grand Teton National Park, we emptied our backpacks and stared at a towering mound of colorful wrappers from single-use snacks. Back in Colorado, we typically skied in the backcountry once, maybe twice a week. Eating "science food," as we like to call packaged foods, wasn't a huge deal then—in fact, it was a really convenient way to get enough calories for what we wanted to do in the mountains. But after

*A snowy day lady shred at Saddleback Ski Resort, Maine (Photo by Katie Lozancich)*

*A sunny groomer day at Jackson Hole Mountain Resort, Wyoming*

several seasons of satiating our ever-increasing appetite for powder turns in the Tetons, we knew that gummy bears, energy gels, and protein bars that vaguely tasted of chocolate weren't going to cut it anymore.

Much like volunteering to flip pancakes for our groggy friends snuggled up in sleeping bags on the floor of a yurt in Colorado, inviting our ski partners and coworkers over for dinner was how we connected with new friends. We frequently maxed out the occupancy limit of our five-hundred-square-foot studio apartment hosting dinner parties, friends squeezed onto our miniature couch or crowded together on the floor with plates in their laps.

We loved the skid life, but we wanted to step it up just a little bit. That was the impetus for our first cookbook, *Beyond Skid: A Cookbook for Ski Bums*, in which we dove into making home cooking accessible for those who dedicate their lives to chasing powder and don't have the time, energy, or budget to enjoy creative and well-balanced meals. In a town like Jackson, where ordering a burger and a beer costs no less than thirty dollars, cooking your own food is crucial to surviving. And it's a lot easier than it looks.

A few years after publishing our first book, we knew we needed to bring that same ethos to fueling on the go. Cooking up a delicious meal after an opic powder day is important, yes, but what about all those calories we need during the six to eight hours we're actually skiing?

As is the case with all good recipes, most of ours began by throwing a bunch of stuff into a food processor to see what would happen. One of our first recipes for portable snacks, our Double-Shot Mocha Energy Balls, is what originally prompted our motivation to write a whole book on fueling for skiing. We both love chocolate. And we *love* espresso. So we tossed a bunch of dates and grains into a food processor along with cocoa and instant espresso powder and crafted what still today is probably our favorite skintrack snack. We fed these mocha-espresso snacks to friends, posted the recipe on our website, and shared it in a few magazines. Soon enough, we ran into friends on the skintrack who told us they'd made our energy balls, and we started wondering how many other ski treats we could come up with.

As we've experimented in the kitchen, the natural progression was to start bringing as much tasty food as we could into the snow with us. Yes, there's the added benefit that everything you eat outdoors tastes a gazillion times better, but having homemade food on the trail really

*Aprés on the deck at the Branca Alpine Hut in Italy. Many of Lily and Max's favorite ski snacks are inspired by their ski trips in the Alps.*

**14 SKI SNACKS**

enhances the entire experience. We ate more frequently, felt more satiated, and once we'd developed a reputation for bringing enough baked goods to share, we got invited on a lot of ski tours. Be careful, though; if you set the standard of offering cake to your ski partners on every outing, the expectations might get out of hand.

Neither of us has any sort of formal culinary background, but that's the point. We've learned almost everything we know in the kitchen from trial and error (*a lot* of error) and lessons from our parents. Max strives to be as in touch with flavors as his dad, who has cooked some of the best food he's ever eaten, though Max has never actually seen him use a cookbook in the kitchen. We read any cookbook we can get our hands on, love trying new foods in new places, and frequent grocery stores whenever we travel. You never know what you'll find around the next aisle.

## SKI SNACKING IS ALL ABOUT TRIAL AND ERROR

This cookbook may make it look like we've got it all figured out, but there have certainly been some not-so-glamorous moments along the way. One November, not long after college, we planned a trip to ski Pico de Orizaba (Citlaltépetl), the highest peak in Mexico and the third highest peak in North America. It was a fast-paced, disorganized trip, with just barely enough time to fly in, climb the mountain, and spend a day in Mexico City. While we spent plenty of time dreaming of the street tacos we'd enjoy post-ski, our "plan" for eating on the mountain left a lot to be desired. In fact, calling it a plan is generous.

We landed late in the evening, crammed our ski bags into a rental car, and drove into the mountains. Close to midnight, we realized we were armed with only a handful of energy bars, and likely wouldn't find an open grocery store in the small town of Tlachichuca, where we'd stay before getting a ride up to basecamp the next day. We pulled off at the only open shop we could find and deliriously bought everything we thought we'd need for the next three days. That poor planning left us with limited options, and we ended up sustaining ourselves mostly on bagged frijoles (surprisingly delicious for the first two meals) and a family-sized carton of Mexican Frosted Flakes.

Plenty went wrong on that trip—lack of snow, zero time to acclimate to the almost nineteen thousand feet of elevation, police checkpoints, and lugging our heavy ski bags through a bustling city on a Friday night—

*Fueling up with a slice of Lemon Yogurt Cake before an evening skate ski in Teton Canyon. (Photo by Zach Montes)*

*Hauling a full pack (with plenty of snacks) on an overnight traverse through the Tetons*

but we still dwell on how horribly we fed ourselves on that mountain. There's no doubt that better food would have helped prevent at least one or two meltdowns.

That was in 2017, and we haven't made a culinary mistake like it on a ski trip since. (We have, however, made plenty of other culinary mistakes, like forgetting to add sugar to a cake, burning the crap out of a tray of brownies while taking a bath, and forgetting an entire bag of food in the car.)

Perhaps the best we've ever eaten on skis has been on our many trips to the Alps. Max is from Germany, and his roots in the Alps run deep, including a summer he spent living and working in Austria at a mountain hut. Lily studied Italian in college and lived in Italy for six months, where she discovered the magic of indulging in alpine meals while skiing in the Ortler mountains.

After college, we returned to the Ortler together with high expectations. One day, on a five-day hut-to-hut traverse of the Ortler Route, a heavy April storm dropped two feet of snow across the glaciated valleys surrounding the Rifugio Pizzini, which had been our home for the first two nights of the trip. All of the terrain is well above tree line, and whiteout conditions took skiing in the alpine off the table for the day. We did, however, need to make it across the valley to the next hut, which would take us at least twice as long with almost zero visibility. We inched along, arduously breaking trail through knee-deep snow, checking the map every few minutes to make sure we were still on track. We could barely see the skis on our feet, and after two hours, we were exhausted. We decided to detour to a small hut, which was closed to overnight guests but offered pastries and espresso to day-trippers. We collapsed into a booth while the storm raged outside the steamy wood-framed windows. Warm slices of apple strudel and cappuccinos breathed new life into us. Thirty minutes later, we walked back into the blizzard with a rejuvenated sense of motivation and an appreciation for how essential a mid-ski slice of cake is—ideally consumed on a wooden deck overlooking a sea of jagged, snowcapped peaks, of course, but just as rejuvenating when wrapped in foil and carefully tucked into a pocket on any trail.

Many of the recipes in *Ski Snacks* are inspired by the incredible food we've enjoyed on the go while skiing around the world. The book in your hands is the effort of two humble North American ski bums to bring the tastes of the world's best pastries and on-the-go meals to skintracks in the States—perhaps in a slightly more portable form than an ultra-flaky croissant, though we love that too.

While not everyone is fortunate enough to spend six or seven days a week on snow, many of us can relate to the not-so-unique struggles of the ski bum. We're busy, tired, and trying not to spend our money exuberantly. We want to try new recipes, but we don't have time to sort through the millions of trendy recipes on the internet. We're sick of store-bought snacking options. Or maybe we just want a creative way to eat more vegetables on the go. Sound familiar?

You don't have to be a hardcore skier to enjoy this compilation of recipes. There are innumerable ways to get out and enjoy snow-covered landscapes, and we have treats to go with all of them. All you need is an open mind, a bit of counter space, and a sense of adventure. While we spend most of our days ski touring in the backcountry or taking advantage of the world-class ski resorts close by, you'll also find us out fat biking, Nordic skiing, or enjoying a nice long walk in the woods—all with a picnic in tow, of course. In fact, it doesn't even need to actually be winter for these recipes to be delicious (although we don't recommend taking things like our Chocolate Dipped Pocket Bacon on a hot summer mountain bike ride or trail run). You have permission to enjoy them any time, whether or not you're sliding on snow.

What we've learned is that there are far better ways to eat than just packaged snacks. So mix it up a bit by adding some fresh ingredients and spice up your next trip into the mountains.

## TAKING CARE OF EACH OTHER IN THE MOUNTAINS

The ski bum life is glorified in many ways. Endless powder days, skipping work to ski, waking up surrounded by mountains that many folks visit for just a few days a year, it's a dream life, but one with high highs and low lows. Since we're writing a book celebrating this magnificent lifestyle—which truly is worth celebrating—it feels remiss to not mention the sometimes dark reality of living in a mountain town. Making ends meet here is more challenging than ever, and it's undeniably far more accessible to those born into a tremendous amount of privilege.

Some days truly are filled only with carefree powder turns and parking-lot beers, but there are plenty of days spent stressing about the rising cost of living, housing insecurity, mountain accidents, or the competitive nature of living in a place surrounded by superhuman athletes. The overwhelming euphoria and fast-paced life in the mountains can be lonely for those struggling with mental health, which doesn't fare well inside a rampant party culture. Taking care of each other is crucial. While there are many ways to show the people in your life how much you care about them, food happens to be our love language. We're not saying a delicious sandwich can solve the ever-worsening housing crisis, but we do believe that food has the power to bring people together. Some of our richest experiences in the Tetons were not the lines we skied but the tasty meals we enjoyed with the people who have become our mountain family.

*There's no backyard like the Tetons. Climbing toward Grand Targhee Mountain Resort after an overnight ski tour between Jackson Hole Mountain Resort and Grand Targhee.*

TWO HUNGRY SKIERS 23

# MAKING YOUR OWN SNACKS

"Science food," as we like to call it, has made our lives a heck of a lot easier. A granola bar between meetings, a handful of candy on the skintrack—we've all been there. But it can be challenging to get *enough* to eat while chasing powder and exploring snowy places.

Moving through the mountains in the winter puts high calorie demands on our bodies, and if you're getting all those calories from packaged foods, that's a lot of wasteful plastic and foil packaging and a lot of the same kinds of offerings.

The two of us spend tons of time outside in the winter, both for work and play, which requires that we eat on an hourly basis to avoid bonking. After exhaustively sampling pretty much every snack out there, we realized that making our own snacks was a healthier, more inspired, and surprisingly easy alternative. Better yet, it turned out to be really fun.

The first time you blitz up a batch of energy balls or bake two dozen miniature cakes, the process might feel excessive, even unwarranted. It's time spent in the kitchen when you could be doing anything else. But when you whip out a Halloumi and Harissa Sandwich or a Bacon and Date Rice Bar in the middle of a snowy tour and your friends literally start drooling, all that work will pay off.

Set yourself up for success and efficiency by establishing a routine, choosing snacks you can batch and prep ahead of time, and giving yourself plenty of time to make them. If you already find cooking and baking fun, then we don't need to keep preaching to you. If you're daunted, fear not! We've got your back.

*Opposite: Enjoying a Powder Day Turkey Club sandwich*
*at the base of a ski line in the Teton Range*

# WHAT MOTIVATES US

I'm always hungry. I (Lily) live in fear of leaving the house for longer than thirty minutes without a snack (whether it's for a few laps at the local ski hill or a few errands around town) and have spent most of my adult life trying to insert delicious bites of food into pretty much everything I do. Luckily, skiing makes me even hungrier, so there's ample opportunity to experiment with tasty flavors and portable skintrack snacks.

I (Max) am actually usually hungrier than Lily, though I've learned to cope with being (slightly) farther away from food. For me, the connection between traveling through the mountains and delicious food was made as a kid hiking and climbing throughout the Alps with my dad and grandfather, where no summit push was without the requisite stop at a mountain hut to refuel.

Making our own snacks opened up a whole new world of possibilities for what kind of food can be enjoyed in the mountains. For the record, our definition of a "snack" might be a bit broader than most. To us, it's anything not eaten as part of a traditional meal—it can be on the chairlift, in the car on the way to the mountain, high atop a hard-earned summit deep in the backcountry, or even back home in the kitchen after a long day harvesting pow turns.

We began toting dinner leftovers, imaginative sandwiches, savory bars, and homemade energy balls and realized that those snacks not only made us feel better, but they also made skiing a whole lot more fun. Taste and smell invoke a powerful sense of nostalgia, and savoring two thick slices of homemade banana bread while enjoying long laps through our favorite trees on Shadow Mountain in Grand Teton National Park definitely sticks with us a little extra thanks to that bite of sweet cinnamony goodness. There's nothing quite like enjoying a homemade baked treat on a snowy summit; it's enjoying the cozy comfort of home while deep in the wilderness.

Traveling abroad to ski has taught us to appreciate the flavors other cultures bring into the mountains—particularly some really good savory ones. With store-bought snacks, we always felt like we were missing out on salty options, so we made Cheesy Polenta Bars and Schnitzel Strips to satisfy our savory tooth. On a ski trip to Japan, we discovered the perfection of pocket onigiri on a cold powder day. The world gets a lot bigger when everything's on the table.

The fact is, the better your food, the more you'll eat. The more you eat, the better you feel—voilà! Your ski day is now significantly better.

*Booting up for a skate ski in Teton Canyon (Photo by Zach Montes)*

MAKING YOUR OWN SNACKS 27

At home, we try to make snack prep fun by streaming a good podcast or jamming out to Beyoncé's country album. Lily likes to call her mom and chat with her on speaker phone while baking treats for our upcoming adventures. Max is always on the hunt for new music when he's cooking. You'll quickly learn that the hour or two you set aside to prep snacks for your winter outings has the potential to become your favorite time of the week! That's certainly been true for us. Aside from skiing, of course. . . Always skiing . . .

## NO NEED TO SWEAR OFF *ALL* PACKAGED SNACKS

We admit we've occasionally taken homemade snacking too far. One time, while getting ready for a multi-week ski trip in the Pacific Northwest, Lily spent the better part of two days whipping up creations for the skintrack: baking quick breads, chilling homemade bars, and stacking sandwiches in the cooler. We had pounds and pounds of homemade snacks and meals, only to realize that on a multiday trip, the weight and bulk really add up. While we're definitely proponents of incorporating homemade snacks on multiday trips as much as possible, it may be necessary to tone it down if weight and space are concerns. Prepackaged snacks can sometimes be the right call—well supplemented by a few of your favorite homemade treats! Everything in moderation, including moderation. Also, we love candy! Sometimes nothing hits the spot quite like a Snickers. Or gummy bears, which Max religiously carried in his ski parka pocket while learning to ski. In fact, Max still clings to his childhood dream of a sponsorship from a candy company. You won't find any snack shamers over here.

The recipes in this book are all designed to *enhance* your experience in the snow, not weigh you down (physically or metaphorically). Our goal is to make ski snacking more fun and creative, not to give you homework. Do what's fun, enjoy your food, and remember to take the time to have a picnic.

Skiing and eating are two of life's greatest gifts. What could be better than combining them?

# STOCKING THE PANTRY

A well-stocked pantry is a glorious sight, like a pristine slope of untouched powder. Well, almost. We're not going to pretend we'd rather stay home organizing our fridge and kitchen cabinets while our friends harvest fresh pow turns, but we admit it brings a certain level of satisfaction. Maybe that means we're growing up.

Having all the supplies you need already on hand makes it easier than ever to whip up a quick ski snack when you make last minute ski plans. There's nothing like an added trip to the store to rob you of your momentum in the kitchen. To get you started, here are the items we tend to stock regularly.

**Spices and seasonings:** Salt is probably the most important ingredient in this book. As folks who love to play in the mountains, our bodies are frequently robbed of salt, so we try to make up for it with well-seasoned food. While you could go crazy with all the different salt options out there, there are two varieties we recommend keeping on hand: kosher salt and flake salt. Kosher salt for baking and general seasoning and flake salt for garnishing. A box of Maldon Sea Salt Flakes will become your secret weapon in the kitchen. Sprinkle it on brownies or chocolate chip cookies for a serious level up.

Spice rack basics include cinnamon, turmeric, ginger, and red pepper flakes. Cocoa powder and instant espresso powder will do wonders to any chocolaty recipe. Add some vanilla bean pods to the mix if you want to be a little bougie. We recommend buying spices more frequently in small quantities to prioritize freshness.

**Oils and butter:** Coconut oil (refined if you don't want a coconutty flavor) and unsalted butter are our two go-tos for cooking, as well as extra-virgin olive oil. Feel free to use coconut oil and butter interchangeably.

**Grains:** Rolled oats (gluten-free if necessary) are definitely among our top five most utilized pantry items. Calrose rice is another important one, both for our rice bars and onigiri recipes. Our cabinets are packed with a plethora of flours, including all-purpose, whole wheat, and spelt flour; as well as gluten-free flours, such as oat flour, almond flour, polenta, and sweet glutinous rice flour (for Butter Mochi).

**Nuts and seeds:** The more the merrier! We love variety. Our pantry is usually stocked with almonds (whole and sliced), walnuts, pistachios, peanuts, and hazelnuts. Seeds we stock include chia, ground flaxseed, and pepitas (a.k.a. pumpkin seeds). Nuts and seeds are all easy to sub for each other, so don't fret if you don't have the exact one a recipe calls for. Your flavor might be a little different, but the result should be the same.

**Nut butters:** Peanut butter is a pretty significant part of our diets, but we mix it up sometimes with almond butter or cashew butter for more neutral flavors. Feel free to use your favorite nut butter.

**Sweeteners:** We use a variety of sweeteners in our recipes, including unrefined sweeteners like maple syrup, honey, and coconut sugar, as well as the classics: granulated sugar and brown sugar. Many of these are interchangeable in recipes.

**Chocolate and candy:** Semisweet chocolate chips are a pantry staple in our household, as is a stockpile of dark chocolate bars that are easy to chop up and toss into a cookie dough or use in other baked goods. A handful of candy, for recipes like Trail Mix Chocolate Chip Cookies, is always welcome. Also, we love Snickers bars and tend to keep a few on hand for a grab-and-go snack.

**Dried fruits:** Dates, dates, dates! A magical backcountry snack, delicious on their own and blitzed into treats, dates are a true hero of ski snacking. We spend a good chunk of our monthly income on dates, #noregrets. Other dried fruits we typically keep on hand for stirring into cookies and blending into energy balls include dried cherries, raisins, and figs.

**Types of milk:** Max is a big whole milk fan, so we've always got a small container of cow's milk in the fridge. Lily's stomach can't handle the real stuff, so we alternate between soy, oat, almond, and coconut milks for smoothies, coffee, and tea. We also keep a handful of full-fat coconut milk cans on hand for baking. If our recipe calls for full-fat coconut milk, we mean it! Otherwise, all other milks can be used interchangeably.

**Canned and jarred goods:** A great jar of jam (homemade if that's your jam) is essential for sandwiches and breakfasts on the go. We also stock the pantry with canned chickpeas, tuna, and black beans for sandwich fillings.

A jar of cornichons or olives can quickly spruce up a sandwich or charcuterie board. We like a mix of green and kalamata olives.

**Meat, eggs, and cheese:** Bacon is one of the main *Beyond Skid* food groups, something you'll notice as you flip through the pages of this book. We love thick-cut bacon, but any will do. As for cured meats, we like to keep prosciutto and salami in the fridge, though it always seems to disappear more quickly than we imagine it might.

We go through tons of eggs in our household, whether for baked goods, breakfast sandwiches, or bite-sized quiches. We try to eat eggs fresh, so we usually end up getting a new carton every time we go to the store. We prefer large eggs—local whenever possible.

Cheese might as well be a whole separate book. We definitely believe most snacks are better with cheese (and lots of it). A nice block of sharp cheddar is probably the most important cheese on hand, ideal for quesadillas, sandwiches, and daily snacking. We also tend to keep goat cheese, brie, mozzarella, parmesan, and feta on hand.

**Condiments:** Having access to an array of condiments is the easiest route to leveling up a sandwich. Our baseline condiments list includes mayonnaise, stone ground mustard, Szechuan-style chili crisp, hot sauce, and Sriracha. If you, like us, enjoy making your own sauces, these items will give you a solid foundation (see chapter 1, Sauces and Spreads).

**Fresh and frozen fruits and veggies:** When you live in a mountain town like we do, you may not have access to a variety of fresh fruits and vegetables year-round. Our freezer is usually stocked with frozen berries for smoothies. For fresh fruit, we keep bananas, apples, and lemons on hand, as well as berries when they're in season. Green onions and salad greens keep pretty well in the fridge, and we keep those on hand to add a little green to whatever sandwich or savory treat we've got cooking.

**Other freezer heroes:** We stash toaster waffles in the freezer for easy sandwiches, as well as any extra sandwich bread we haven't gotten to and want to save from going stale. Puff pastry is handy, too, and about as skid friendly as it gets.

 **SKID HACK:** Use puff pastry to replace any sweet or savory tart crust, for the quickest and tastiest dessert or treat that feels far fancier than it is to prepare.

**Best purchased fresh, as needed:** There's nothing worse than a stale baguette. Baguettes are pretty unforgiving when it comes to the small window in which you can enjoy them before they go stale, so we try to pick one up no sooner than the day before we plan to eat it. Sliced turkey or ham is also something we buy on an as-needed basis, since neither keeps for more than a few days.

**Specialty:** Some ingredients aren't exactly pantry staples, but they're things we like to keep on hand for specific recipes. Marzipan (or almond paste) stores well in the pantry; we keep a few 7-ounce logs of it with our baking supplies for when a craving strikes for Mini Orange Marzipan Cakes. Similarly, mochiko flour (for Butter Mochi) is harder to find at mountain-town grocery stores, so we order it in bulk online and keep a couple boxes in the pantry.

*Searching for soft turns high above the fjord near Åndalsnes, Norway*

MAKING YOUR OWN SNACKS 33

## AN ODE TO NATURE'S BEST SWEETENER: MAPLE SYRUP

### KATIE LOZANCICH

I never understood the hype around maple syrup until I met my partner, Luke, a true New Englander. One day at the grocery store, I grabbed my go-to, log-cabin-shaped bottle of syrup chock-full of high-fructose corn syrup. Luke recoiled. "No way, absolutely not," he said. "I prefer the authentic stuff from home." Being a naive Californian, I didn't get it. "It can't be that different," I laughed. But one trip to Massachusetts was enough to convince me.

Pure maple syrup, the stuff that takes forty gallons of maple sap for a single gallon of syrup, is something to behold. The flavor is smooth, warm, and nutty. It's sweet, but in a refined way—nothing compared to the sugary rush of a soda or a handful of sour gummy candy. On top of being nature's best sweetener, maple syrup is high in antioxidants, nutrients, and minerals. Go ahead, add it to your coffee every morning. The best maple syrup comes in the most

# TOOLS AND EQUIPMENT

Much like setting out in the backcountry with a beacon, shovel, and probe, it's important to kick off a kitchen project with the right gear. We like to keep our kitchen gadgets pretty minimal (you won't find an air fryer or sous vide on this list). You only need a baseline set of kitchen appliances to put you on a path to success.

We also believe that rules are meant to be broken, so just because you don't have an item we suggest using in the recipe (like a stand mixer), don't feel like you should throw in the towel and ignore that recipe altogether. When possible, we'll suggest alternatives. For example, forks are great banana mashers and so are your hands!

illogical container: an opaque jug with a screw top that always cakes up with crystallized sugar. Every time you pour from it, you have to clean the cap, or it won't close. Make sure the bottle you buy says "Massachusetts" or "Vermont" on the side. The proper form is to acquire an entire gallon, nothing less. Think that's excessive? Think again. You can put it on nearly everything. Maple syrup on Greek yogurt? Done. Brussels sprouts with bacon? Absolutely. Maple with lemon and salt mixed with water for your ski tour? Take that, Gatorade. Better yet, take a teeny bottle on your next adventure and take a round of shots with your friends. Less bite than tequila, way smoother than whiskey.

*Katie Lozancich is a photographer and artist based in western Massachusetts who is passionate about good food and sharing it with friends. Katie credits Max and Lily with learning how to properly cook—and no, they did not bribe her to say that.*

**One really, really good kitchen knife:** Even if you live in a glorified crash pad with eight other ski bums, a sharp, high-quality chef's knife is the one kitchen item you don't want to skimp on. It's kind of like the dichotomy of a ski bum living paycheck to paycheck, cruising around in a dilapidated Subaru from the '90s, but skiing on a two-thousand-dollar ski setup. Priorities. If your budget can swing it, an eight- or nine-inch chef's knife as well as a five-inch chopper will give you ultimate kitchen freedom. And if you really want to go crazy, throw in a serrated knife for bread and tomatoes. Then you'll be living large.

**Measuring cups:** You'll need a standard set of measuring cups and spoons for many of the recipes in this book.

**Mixing bowls:** If you have a set of three bowls: small, medium, and large, you're all set.

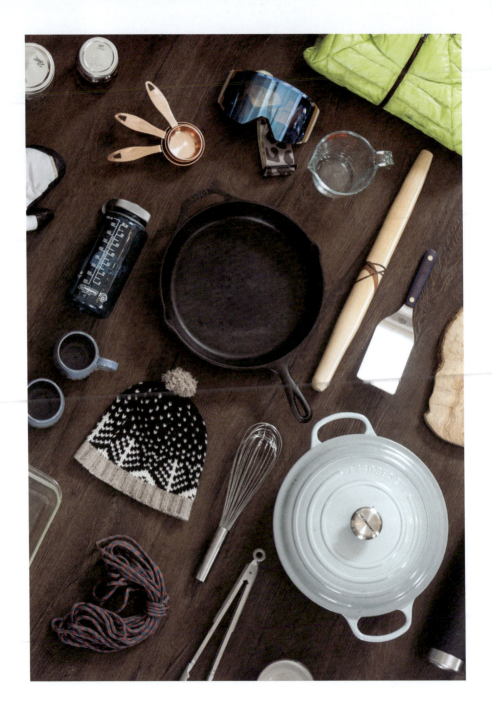

**Pots and pans:** A large cast iron skillet will take you far. So will a non-stick pan for eggs and a few medium saucepans for boiling water.

**Baking sheets and pans:** Two or three full-sized baking sheets are ideal to have in the rotation. An 8-by-8-inch and a 9-by-13-inch baking dish are ideal for recipes like Fudgy Espresso Brownies and Butter Mochi Cake. For loaves, we've got a couple of 8-by-4-inch baking pans.

**Parchment paper:** For lining your baking sheets and pans. Not only does it increase the longevity of your pans, it makes cleanup a breeze!

**Oven thermometer:** Ideal for checking the accuracy of your oven temps. We've burned plenty a baked treat by putting too much trust in our oven's automatic temperature settings.

**Toaster:** Important for toasting bread. If you are one of the few people who does not own a toaster, feel free to toast bread for your sandwiches in a cast iron pan or under the broiler in your oven—but keep a close eye on it! You should probably just buy a toaster.

**Food processor:** Necessary for recipes like Energy Balls and Everyday Pesto. If you're committed to being old fashioned, you could use a mortar and pestle (not recommended).

**Blender:** Nice to have for smoothies, but you can technically use a food processor for anything you need a blender for.

**Resealable plastic bags:** A variety of bags (gallon, quart, and snack size) are essential for storing treats in the fridge or freezer and taking them on the trail (see "How to Package Your Own Snacks").

**Thermos:** Small and large thermoses—depending on your adventure—are key for toting drinks on the trail! Our Sippables chapter features plenty of warm drinks for sipping along the skintrack. We recommend sizes anywhere from a small, 10-ounce up to a 24-ounce shareable thermos. As always, we suggest adapting recipes to the size of the thermos you have, instead of going out and buying a fifty-dollar stainless steel jug.

**SKID HACK:** Don't bother buying a whisk. A fork works just great for the whisking part of any recipe we've ever made.

# NOT HUNGRY?

**KAYLEE PICKETT**

You planned and carefully packed all your snacks for the day. But when you stop for water and food breaks, you can hardly take a bite of anything. What's going on? Why don't you feel hungry?

Exercise can dull hunger and thirst cues. Physical exertion activates the sympathetic nervous system, also known as "fight or flight," prioritizing muscle contraction, quick decision-making, and cardiovascular output. This allows you to push vertical feet and miles on the trail. Extreme heat or cold intensifies its activation.

As a result, the digestive system slows down considerably, and you may not feel hungry for hours, despite high output. In fact, normal digestion can only restart once the body moves out of the sympathetic nervous system and into the parasympathetic nervous system, which is referred to as "rest and digest" because it encourages digestion, muscle and tissue repair, and fluid balance.

But moderate-to-high-intensity activity can increase calorie needs by up to fifty times, so it's important to snack regularly throughout your effort, even if your body is not asking for it. Most people feel their best when they eat a small snack around one hour into the activity and repeat every forty-five to sixty minutes after. Eating every hour or so helps deliver calories to the body in the form of sugar, protein, and fat. Foods that are high in sugar, in the form of carbohydrates, are easier to digest and therefore give you an energy boost right away. Protein and fat help your tissues rebuild and repair during activity and after.

Be sure to sip often, as your hydration needs can double during intense exercise. Water, electrolyte mixes, tea, and drinks, like Salted Maple Lemonade, help keep you hydrated and offer vitamins and minerals that keep you feeling stronger longer.

Remember that the body may stay in its fight-or-flight mode for hours after you leave the trailhead. Continue snacking and sipping regularly to help your body relax and shift into its rest-and-digest system so that you can repair, rebuild, and get ready for your next adventure.

*Kaylee Pickett loves skiing, rock climbing, and trail running almost as much as she loves snacks. In her work as a holistic nutrition counselor, Kaylee focuses on helping people better understand and care for their bodies with an approach to health and nutrition that focuses on mindset, whole (and delicious!) foods, and a lifestyle with holistic wellness at the center.*

*Kaylee Pickett is all smiles on a skintrack in the Tetons.*

MAKING YOUR OWN SNACKS

# HOW TO PACKAGE YOUR OWN SNACKS

Have we sold you on it yet? Perhaps you love the idea of savoring home-made snacks on the slopes but are daunted by how to get them there intact. How do you keep Bribery Banana Bread from crumbling or a Tomato Jam and Arugula Breakfast Sammie from getting smooshed?

We hear you. It's the transporting of the snacks that can feel like the crux of enjoying your own food on the trail. In fact, when quizzing our friends, family, and ski partners over the past few seasons, the packaging of homemade snacks was the biggest obstacle to taking their own food on their outdoor adventures and the reason they opted to buy snacks from the store instead.

Through years of trial and error (many errors), solving the puzzle of how to package treats is a game we've grown to enjoy.

There's no single right way to package snacks, which is part of the fun. There are, however, definitely a few wrong ways. Most of those result in a backpack smeared with jam or crumbs lining your pockets for eternity. We've smooshed, spilled, and pummeled our fair share of food in pursuit of homemade snacking on skis, so hopefully you don't have to repeat our mistakes.

Here are some of our favorite packaging methods, and what we like and don't like about each. We try to be conscious of the waste some of these methods create, since waste was one of the reasons we started replacing individually wrapped, store-bought snacks with our own. Feel free to experiment a bit and figure out what works best for you. Likely, there are options we haven't even thought of, so get creative!

## ALUMINUM FOIL

The structure of aluminum foil can help maintain a snack's shape, especially for recipes like Bacon and Date Rice Bars and slices of Lemon Yogurt Cake. It's also great for Pocket Dillas; since they pack down so darn flat, it's easy to stack quite a few in your pack. But it can be tough to reuse if it tears or gets too crinkled or messy. Paper-backed foil is easier to reuse, as is high-quality, thick aluminum foil. Try to avoid the super-thin foil. Even though it's much cheaper, it will tear open before you even dig into your snack!

**Pros:**
- Lightweight
- Inexpensive
- Helps snacks hold their shape
- Packable

**Cons:**
- Wasteful/harder to reuse
- Not sealable

## RESEALABLE PLASTIC BAGS

Snack-sized, resealable plastic bags can be incredibly useful for ski snacks. They're easy to rinse and reuse, and they don't take up much extra space. They work well for recipes like Chocolate Chairlift Cookies, Quick Candied Nuts, and anything else that might need a seal, like Chocolate-Dipped Pocket Bacon. But no promises that your cookies won't turn to crumbs if you're not careful where you stash these packages of goodness.

**Pros:**
- Lightweight
- Inexpensive
- Packable
- Fully sealable

**Cons:**
- Don't protect fragile snacks
- Wasteful if you don't reuse (can't be reused indefinitely)

## REUSABLE SILICONE BAGS

Silicone bags are super bomber and hold up well while getting tossed around in a gear-filled backpack. We like the sandwich-sized bag for (you guessed it) a lot of our Summit Sandwiches as well as our Trail Mix Chocolate Chip Cookies.

**Pros:**
- Easy to wash and reuse
- Add a little protection/structure
- Fully sealable

**Cons:**
- Single bags are expensive
- Bulky and heavy

## BEESWAX WRAP

We recently started using beeswax-wrapped cotton paper, a fun alternative to foil, to wrap sandwiches and bars, and love how sturdy it is. It works really well for oddly shaped snacks and sammies, like Le Chamoniard Baguette, since it can be folded into whatever shape you'd like. Maximum flexibility!

**Pros:**
- Lightweight
- Molds to whatever shape you need
- Adds some structure and protection

**Cons:**
- Harder to wash
- Not sealable
- More expensive than resealable plastic bags

## TAKEOUT CONTAINERS

Like any good ski bum, we use repurposed plastic takeout containers for most of our food-storage needs. We love the small, cylindrical, 8-ounce containers for transporting Energy Balls and other small bites, since the structure of the container protects them from getting smooshed.

**Pros:**
- Protects fragile snacks
- Fully sealable
- Usually free with a takeout order

**Cons:**
- Bulky
- May need to be washed by hand

## HARD-SIDED PLASTIC CONTAINERS

We use hard-sided containers for fragile snacks, like sandwiches and Cheesy Polenta Bars, and anything with a strong smell (Kimchi Grilled Cheese) that's best sealed off from the rest of our gear.

**Pros:**
- Easy to wash in the dishwasher
- Sturdy protection for fragile snacks
- Fully sealed

**Cons:**
- Bulky
- Heavy

## THE GOODIE BAG

Drawstring-closure skin bags are great for carrying most of your individually packaged snacks in one place inside your backpack, making it really easy to refuel. Zip open your pack and grab all your snacks at once (though we do like to stash some goodies in our pockets for even faster access). Any nylon stuff sack can serve the same purpose—and is washable and reusable.

# WHAT KIND OF SKI SNACKER ARE YOU?

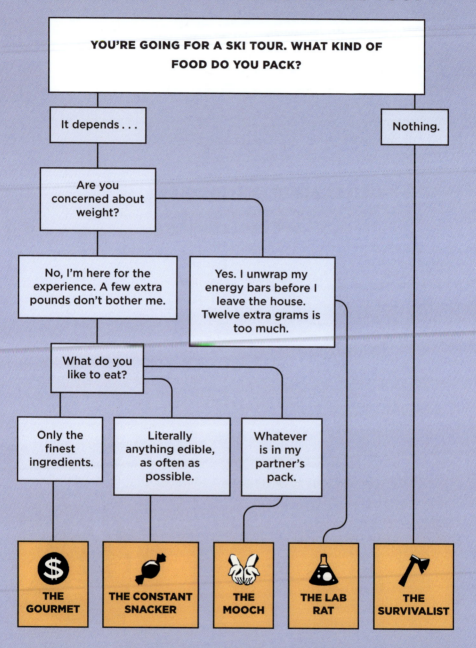

## THE GOURMET

I enjoy the finer things in life. I exclusively wear pricey brand-name clothes. Oh, and I'm gonna need to cut out early today because my sourdough starter needs to be fed. I'm in it for the snacks, but only if it's aged manchego, fresh arugula, and prosciutto crudo on a fresh baguette . . . flown in from Europe. I know it's heavy, but I brought this mason jar of radish pickles that I made last week. How's that for electrolytes?

## THE CONSTANT SNACKER

I'm so hungry I can barely introduce myself. I keep a box of cereal on my nightstand in case I get hangry in my dreams. Every pocket of my ski jacket has a different snack, and I ditched my first aid kit for a Pica's burrito. We should probably stop and have a snack. What is that? Can I have a bite of that?

## THE MOOCH

The first thing I learned in my Avy 1 was to always ski with a partner . . . so they can carry your food and water, right? It's a team effort over here. I'd totally offer to drive, but that overnight parking spot I nabbed last week is just too good to give up. Also, it's my roommate's car. Can I have a small sip of your water? I'll get you back later.

## THE LAB RAT

No snack breaks, I'm here for the fastest known time. GU is the greatest innovation because you can eat it while you walk. Why bother with this cookbook when NASA already has it all figured out? If it comes in a tube, I'm in. Almost all my calories come from a powder, paste, or a pulverized mass of unpronounceable ingredients. I'm basically a robot. An eighteen-liter pack fits everything I need, and I'm ready to get electro*lit*.

## THE SURVIVALIST

I survive off the land, even in the dead of winter. Except, of course, I drove my EarthRoamer to the trailhead, since, you know, it's pretty cold out and I needed a warm place to put my boots on. Other than that, I like to see how far the human body can take me in its natural state. Technology breeds weakness (except for TikTok of course). #fastedtraining only, please.

MAKING YOUR OWN SNACKS 45

# DON'T BONK: TIPS FOR STAYING FUELED

"Lunch starts at the car and ends at the bar." In other words, we start snacking when we leave the parking lot and don't let up until post-ski beers. Lunch is an all-day affair.

These are words we try to live by in regular life, but most importantly during ski season, when our caloric needs are highest. Avoid bonking by following a few simple tips.

**Pack enough.** How long will you be out? Will there be an opportunity to refill water or re-up on snacks? We like to take a little more than we think we'll need so we don't finish our day with a cleaned-out goodie bag. Plus, that means options! Variety is the spice of life. Don't rob yourself of that, even deep in the wilderness.

**Pack a variety.** You're way more likely to eat if you're excited about what's in your pack. We like to take a variety of different foods (a mix of sweet and savory and quick- and slow-burning energy) so that when we're tired or working hard, we can choose what sounds good at the moment.

**Eat frequently.** Sometimes a full-on summit picnic is the vibe we need. But more often than not, it's the frequent, small bites that keep us going in the mountains. On most days, we snack about once an hour, sometimes on the go with accessible pocket snacks, sometimes brief bites while we stop to take a layer off, and sometimes a full-on picnic. Eat a little bit, and repeat. Or eat a lot, on the regular. Don't wait until you're hungry to bust out the snacks (see "Not Hungry?" sidebar).

**Choose ski partners who love to snack.** Different folks have different snacking needs and interests. While there's no right or wrong approach, it can be helpful to discuss your habits beforehand, to set expectations. Is your friend trying out fasted training today? Are you on a time crunch? It matters less what you do and more that everyone's on the same page about fueling.

# THE MEGA SNACK

## JACK BEIGHLE

I've carried a burrito to the top of nearly every Teton summit. Spaghetti and meatballs have accompanied me on many a four-thousand-foot ski tour. When I touted that fact to some of my more pack-weight-conscious amigos, they scoffed. To them, carrying a two-pound burrito into the mountains is irresponsible, and the only way to rectify your error is to get that heavy snack out of your pack and into your stomach ASAP. To me, that's just plain wrong. Every day in the mountains should be accompanied by at least one snack big enough to be considered a meal: the Mega Snack.

But when is the best time to consume that delectable burrito, pizza, or sandwich? Where will you enjoy it the most? Is it when you're most hungry? Or do you wait until the summit or high point of the day? If you, like me, go to the mountains purely for the enjoyment of being there, then yes, if the views are nice at the summit, the sun is out, and the window of safety isn't rapidly diminishing, park yourself on a rock and chow down. However, things often don't go to plan.

Maybe the wind is honking at your chosen high point. Maybe you're tired and just want to get down. Maybe your buddy is going to get impatient and pester you for the entirety of your sandwich consumption. You may need to consider an alternate plan.

If you feel that your enjoyment will be maximized at the moment you're the hungriest, then follow your heart. If you'd rather eat last night's pad thai under a nice tree, then do it up. And if, for some horrible, no good, masochistic reason, you would rather leave your favorite snack at the car to be enjoyed later, then, I guess, that is your right.

So bring that pulled pork sandwich to the top of your next ski descent. Carry a whole pizza to the highest point you've ever skied from. Whatever you do, enjoy it.

*Jack Beighle of Boulder, Colorado, loves burritos. He especially loves them on tall mountains in the Tetons. If they explode in his backpack, he loves them less.*

# HOW TO USE THIS BOOK

Whether you're a ski bum shopping on a budget with three square feet of kitchen countertop or a seasoned home cook with a myriad of ingredients at your fingertips, we hope you'll find recipes within this book that become your go-to fuel for adventures in the mountains.

There's something for everyone in this cookbook. You'll find sauces and spreads in chapter 1 to spice up your sandwich or charcuterie board, trailside or inside. The Quick Bites chapter offers a range of simple snacks you can pull out of your pocket and eat on the go with minimal fanfare, like Energy Balls or Candied Spiced Nuts.

And you'll find larger portions too, like in the Summit Sandwiches chapter, because spending time in the mountains calls for a whole lotta calories, and sometimes a Bacon-Wrapped Date or Pocket Onigiri just isn't going to cut it. We're big proponents of the Mega Snack and transporting anything celebratory to pat yourself on the back (or stomach?) for a job well done. A Powder Day Turkey Club is always worth the weight—a classic that needs no further persuasion. And creative summit meals, like our Grilled Halloumi and Harissa Sandwich, are great ways to brag about your refined palette.

The Baked Goods chapter offers sweet treats, like Mini Orange Marzipan Cakes and Handheld Apfelstrudel, that pay homage to our love for skiing in the Alps. While the Lemon Yogurt Cake is just a great excuse to eat more cake for breakfast. The Sippables chapter busts the narrative that we need to buy expensive manufactured drink mixes, by offering alternatives made from natural ingredients you likely already have in the pantry, to whip up recipes like Miso Honey-Lemon Water and Carrot Ginger Soup—yes, we sip soup!

*Opposite: Meals in the snow on the shore of Jackson Lake, Wyoming,*
*during an overnight spring ski trip*

And though we love to snack on the go, sometimes a beautiful bluebird day is just begging for a high-mountain picnic. Maybe that means hauling your favorite snacks up to a scenic perch, or maybe it's stocking the car with all the fixings for a sunny parking-lot hang. Bask in the glory of your day with plenty of sustenance waiting for you in the car. For these occasions, turn to the Tailgate Treats chapter, where you'll find our favorite charcuterie fixings, reasons why you should, indeed, bring your pizza oven to the trailhead, and simple smoothie recipes that require only a brief shake before sipping.

We're not the only ones who can go on and on about the power of eating delicious food in the snow, though. While putting together these recipes, we reached out to fellow skiers—industry professionals, nutritionists, devoted ski bums, and lovers of all things snow—to get their take on snacking while skiing. We whipped up their creations in our own little kitchen, and sprinkled their recipes and musings on winter food throughout the book. Because just like skiing, food is all about community.

*Finding soft pockets of snow at Jackson Hole Mountain Resort*

# RECIPE RATINGS

If you have spent time sliding down snow on skis or a snowboard, our recipe ratings will likely look familiar. Like ski runs in North America, we've broken down the difficulty ratings of our recipes into green, blue, and black "runs." If you're feeling intimidated by technical kitchen supplies, "pizza" your way down a green recipe to start. Or go full send and bomb down a black recipe to get the blood pumping.

Warm up with these simple ski-bum-friendly recipes. Our green runs are our easiest recipes. They don't have a ton of ingredients, appliances, or prep work. They're the kind of recipe that boosts your ego, much like laying down turns on fresh, low-angle corduroy.

A step up from the bunny hill, blue runs, or recipes, get easier the more you attempt them. Once you're in the flow, you'll be able to cruise down these slopes with your brain (mostly) turned off.

For the adventurous home chef, drop into some of our more complex recipes. These recipes may require more steps, specialized tools, or just unusual ingredients. They might look technical and intimidating at first, but you'll be rewarded with some truly unique skintrack snacks.

# ALPINE PICNICS

The summer of my (Max's) junior year in high school, my dad and I walked across the Alps from Germany to Italy. That two-week trip marked a turning point in my life, one where I knew I needed to pursue a lifestyle that, above all, gave me access to mountains. You might think that what stood out most from the trip was long days on the trail, vistas from high peaks, or overcoming technical challenges with my dad—but to be honest, what I remember the most was what we ate.

We still talk about specific meals we had on that trip and our realization that our north-to-south trajectory came with the added bonus that the food consistently got better day by day. Germans have it pretty figured out, the Austrians have refined it, and the Italians revel in the fact that they've turned Alpine cuisine into an art form.

We spent every day on the move (save for one trapped at a beautiful mountain hut on a glacier in an August snowstorm feasting on *Kaiserschmarrn* and lentil soup), walking up and down peaks, and stopping daily in small Alpine villages on the valley floor to restock. The thing about the Alps is that, while they are among the most stunningly beautiful ranges on the planet, they are actually not that wild—it's easy to get locally made sausages, cheeses, breads, wine, and other goodies literally *everywhere.*

March into a tiny town glued to a precipitous hillside, find the local market or butcher, and you'll quickly source some of the best food in the world. All for just a few euros. We fueled ourselves for two weeks from what we found locally, knowing that the farmers, butchers, bakers, and snack makers were equally invested in the lifestyle that I had just fallen in love with. That sentiment has only grown stronger since then, fueling my desire to experience the mountains at a slower pace, stopping to smell the baked goods, and sharing my love for real food in wild places with the people I love.

*Max and his dad, Gerd, on a fall hiking trip in the Catskills of New York, a few years before their Alpine adventure. Hiking with his parents shaped Max's perspective on food and the mountains.*

HOW TO USE THIS BOOK

## THE BEST INGREDIENTS ARE THE ONES YOU HAVE

If you live in a landlocked mountain town, chances are you don't have a plethora of fresh ingredients readily available year round. Here in the Tetons, it's slim pickings for local produce in the middle of winter. Some of our recipes call for fresh fruits or vegetables that you might not have access to year-round, but fear not. We often lean on frozen fruits and berries from the grocery store or from our own freezer, where we stockpile summer and fall fruits when we're able.

Our recipes are inherently flexible, designed to use ingredients that are (mostly) easy to track down, if not already in your pantry. Often we decide on our recipes after we've taken stock of our fridge and pantry, so starting with what you have on hand will make your grocery list a whole lot shorter. There's no single right way to make your way down a slope. Similarly, there's no single right way to make any of these recipes. Consider these recipes loose guidelines, but use common sense (we don't want to hear complaints if you swapped in tuna for hazelnuts and didn't like the taste of your Homemade Nutella).

Also, feel free to omit or swap out a fresh ingredient completely if it doesn't feel right. We'll skip the tomato on a sandwich if all that's available is a pale, mealy tomato trucked in from halfway across the world. Just like choosing where to ski based on conditions, choosing what to snack on should depend on what looks good at the grocery store.

# COOKING AT ALTITUDE

We live at an altitude of a little over six thousand feet and have tested and developed all of our recipes here. To be totally honest, the whole "cooking at altitude" topic is one we don't worry much about. There are a lot of techy answers in America's Test Kitchen and all over the internet, but in general, we just, well . . . ignore it.

We've had friends and family test our recipes, both at sea level and higher up in the Rockies, and they didn't do much in the way of substitutions. That's not to say the science isn't legit. It's just to say that our whole philosophy to cooking and prepping snacks is based on a lack of precision. It's a bit of a loose operation over here. Luckily, a lot of our recipes don't involve much cooking at all!

You might find that you need to bake loaves or cookies for a little longer or a little shorter depending on where you live, so a lot of our recipes in the Baked Goods chapter start with a low suggestion for bake time, with the idea that you can always bake for longer, but you can't go back in time if you bake for too long.

In high and dry climates like the Tetons (and even more so in Colorado), baked goods dry out much more quickly than in humid climates at sea level. Keeping quick breads, cookies, and bars in a sealed container is essential if you want them to last for more than a day or two. You can also freeze baked items if you are concerned you won't eat them fast enough.

*Snack testing during a powder day on Teton Pass*

# SAUCES AND SPREADS

When Max was a little kid, he learned about the role of the saucier in classical restaurant kitchens, and for a while it became his dream job. Turns out the right sauce is what makes a good recipe excellent, whether it's a fancy meal on a night out or that triple-stacked sandwich you just devoured on top of a hard-earned summit. We're allergic to boring tastes, so we compiled some of our favorite simple sauces that will make any sandwich, pizza, or quick bite that much better. Feel free to just eat these by the spoonful . . . we won't judge.

These essential sauces and spreads appear time and again throughout the book. We lather Everyday Pesto on any sandwich we can and toss it with pasta for quick, twenty-minute dinners. Aioli is a kitchen superhero, one that Max believes should go on literally everything . . . much to Lily's chagrin. And when you're feeling fancy (because yes, you deserve it!), whip up your very own Homemade Nutella and add chocolate to toast, fruit, waffles, and yogurt.

Most of these sauces and spreads can be made in bulk and kept in the fridge to have ready whenever the need for a snack arises, on or off the mountain.

*Opposite: Looking out across the Selkirk Mountains on a week-long lodge trip in British Columbia*

# AIOLI, THREE WAYS

More than just the "glue" of sandwiches, a good aioli adds a kick of flavor to your favorite portable. Think of it as fancy mayo that will elevate anything it goes on. It's really quick to make, from ingredients you probably already have around, and can be spiced up any number of ways. Keep aioli in the fridge for up to a week so you're always ready when the snow starts stacking up and there's no time for anything but skiing pow.

**Makes about 1 cup**

### FOR THE BASE

2 egg yolks

2 cloves garlic, finely chopped

1 teaspoon kosher salt

⅔ cup extra-virgin olive oil

### CLASSIC GARLIC

1 additional clove garlic, finely chopped

1 teaspoon lemon juice (preferably freshly squeezed, but bottled lemon juice will suffice)

### HONEY DIJON

1 tablespoon honey

1 tablespoon dijon mustard

### SPICY

1 tablespoon hot sauce (such as Sriracha or another Asian chili sauce)

In a large bowl, whisk together the egg yolks, garlic, and salt until well combined.

Slowly add the olive oil while vigorously whisking until it becomes stiff.

Whisk in the rest of the ingredients, adjusting to taste.

Refrigerate in a sealed container until ready to use.

# EVERYDAY PESTO

We've been tweaking this recipe for years. Though it always looks a little different depending on what kind of greens we have on hand, a few crucial components always stay the same: we toast the garlic alongside the nuts and add white miso paste for a kick of umami.

Feel free to substitute any nut for the almonds and walnuts here. If you've got the cash to shell out for pine nuts, you can make this pesto a little more traditional. For now, we'll be sticking with the dirtbag-friendly, kale-almond-walnut version. Or even better: Use radish or beet greens that typically get thrown out. Bonus dirtbag points if you don't have to pay for them.

---

**Makes about 1 cup**

¼ cup + 1 tablespoon extra-virgin olive oil, divided

⅓ cup mixed almonds and walnuts

1 to 2 cloves garlic, sliced in half

2 teaspoons white miso paste

2 cups greens and/or herbs (such as kale, basil, radish greens, beet greens, or a mix of everything)

1 teaspoon lemon juice

¼ teaspoon kosher salt

Heat a pan to medium-high and add ¼ cup of the olive oil.

Toast the nuts and garlic on the stove until they become fragrant. Watch them closely; they'll go from lightly toasted to burnt in about a millisecond.

Add the garlic, nuts, miso paste, and remaining 1 tablespoon of olive oil to a food processor or high-speed blender and blend on high for about 20 seconds.

Add the greens, lemon juice, and salt, then process again.

Keep processing until you've reached your desired consistency. Add salt to taste. For a more easily spreadable pesto, add olive oil as needed to achieve desired consistency.

Store in an airtight container in the fridge for up to one week.

SAUCES AND SPREADS 61

# SUNDRIED TOMATO AND OLIVE TAPENADE

This is probably the fanciest sauce in this book, but once you discover that you can source most of the ingredients from the deli bar and canned-foods aisle in your average grocery store, this Mediterranean-inspired delight is quick and painless to make. The salty and tangy flavor is great on sandwiches, pizza, or just on its own as part of a charcuterie board. Lily once had the best baguette sandwich of her life in the Zurich airport. It was lathered with a sundried tomato and olive tapenade just like this. And every time we enjoy this sauce with a hunk of good bread, it takes us back to skiing in the Alps.

**Makes about 1 cup**

2 cups pitted kalamata olives, drained

3 cloves garlic, smashed

⅓ cup sundried tomatoes, drained

Add the olives, garlic, tomatoes, and basil to a food processor and pulse until you've achieved a coarse texture, 15 to 20 seconds.

Slowly add in the olive oil and pulse again.

⅓ cup chopped fresh basil, tightly packed

2 tablespoons extra-virgin olive oil

2 tablespoons lemon juice

Sprinkle of flake salt

Sprinkle of ground black pepper

Add the lemon juice, salt, and pepper. Pulse again. Season to taste.

Spread on a toasted baguette or store in a sealed container in the fridge for up to a week.

# LEARNING WHAT *YOUR* BODY NEEDS

### KYRA FOLEY

It really wasn't until about a decade into my love for hiking, climbing, and skiing that I realized I was consistently under-eating for the activities I wanted to do. Whether it was stigma around women's bodies, embarrassment for getting a third serving, or really just being uneducated on how many calories I needed to sustain my body, I just wasn't eating enough. Many of my male climbing and skiing partners rarely packed more than a few beef jerky sticks and some candy, so I followed suit, assuming I needed less food than men twice my size. It was extremely validating when other women showed me how important it was to bring enough food to fuel and that it was okay if I needed more snacks than my male partners. This changed everything for me. What still sometimes feels like overindulging now leaves me satiated with energy to spare.

Snack before you feel the bonk, and that extra pound of food in your pack is seriously worth it. Every body is different, regardless of gender, and the amount and type of food it takes to help you move the way you want to is so unique. I'm still learning.

*Kyra Foley of Jackson, Wyoming, loves to eat pasta outside, usually accompanied by muddy dogs and a Highpoint cider (see her Eat Pasta Ski Fasta recipe). She learned how to ski at Jackson Hole Mountain Resort as a young lassie, and now enjoys silly laps on Teton Pass, skijoring, and wild ice skating.*

# MISO PEANUT SAUCE

This sauce dates back to the very origins of *Beyond Skid*. It's a year-round staple in our kitchen—our all-time favorite sauce for noodle dishes, rice bowls, sandwiches, and spring rolls. We love it so much that we almost suggested it as a sippable electrolyte drink, but reined ourselves in and decided it may be best left as a sauce or spread. We keep a jar of this sauce in the fridge at all times because it's an easy way to zhuzh up whatever we've got simmering. It also freezes well. We like to make an extra big batch and pour it into silicone freezer trays in one-cup or half-cup increments.

**Makes about 1 cup**

¼ cup creamy peanut butter

3 tablespoons warm water

2 tablespoons white miso paste

1 tablespoon rice vinegar

1 tablespoon honey

1 teaspoon soy sauce

¼ teaspoon kosher salt

¼ teaspoon ground ginger

Add all ingredients to a blender and blend until smooth. If the sauce is too thick, add a dash of warm water.

Store in a sealed container in the fridge for up to two weeks or in the freezer for up to six months.

# QUICK PLUM RHUBARB JAM

Scraped the last morsel of jam out of your jar for yesterday's PB&J? Make a homemade quick jam. These jams are some of our favorite ways to bring a little sweetness to a sandwich, which are excellent to snack on while skiing. We stock up on spring and summer produce and stash it in the freezer for the cold, dark days of winter. Simmering frozen fruit into something spreadable is an easy way to bring it back to life.

Small batches are usually our go-to, since they don't require the intimidating process of canning and preserving. As long as you enjoy the jam within a month or so, it should keep just fine in the fridge. We opted for sweet plums and tart rhubarb for this quick jam, but feel free to experiment with whatever you've got or can pick up from the frozen aisle of the grocery store.

**Makes about 1 cup**

3 cups chopped frozen rhubarb

1 cup frozen plum halves

¼ cup water, plus more as needed

¼ cup maple syrup, plus more to taste

1 teaspoon ground cinnamon

Pinch of kosher salt

Add the fruit and water to a small saucepan and heat to medium-high until it's bubbling.

Lower the heat and let the mix simmer uncovered until the fruit starts to break down, 10 to 15 minutes.

Add 1 tablespoon of water at a time, using a fork or spoon to mash the fruit until the whole mixture thins out to the consistency of a chunky tomato sauce.

Stir in the maple syrup, cinnamon, and salt and cook for another 10 minutes or so, until the jam thickens to your desired consistency.

Pour into a jar and let cool on the counter.

Seal and store in the fridge for three to four weeks. It might keep longer, but we always finish it up too fast to find out!

SAUCES AND SPREADS

# HOMEMADE NUTELLA

Store-bought Nutella is delicious. We aren't going to argue with that. It's one of those treats that is best enjoyed while turning a blind eye to the ingredient list, which of course is easy to do when it's already lathered on a croissant or a golden-brown waffle.

Lily first set out to make her own version while she was avoiding dairy and determined to enjoy a dairy-free version of the chocolate-hazelnut spread everyone on the planet seems to love so much. We may be a little biased, but we think our version is far tastier than the store-bought version. This recipe dispenses with the sugar and palm oil that make up most of the standard version and doubles up on hazelnuts and chocolate. More of the good stuff, less of the not-so-good stuff. If you can find hazelnut extract, that will take it over the top. Spread it on a waffle or sandwich for the road, dip strawberries in it for dessert, or eat it by the spoonful.

**Makes about 1.5 cups**

2 cups raw hazelnuts

2 tablespoons walnut or vegetable oil, plus more as needed

½ cup cocoa powder

1 teaspoon vanilla extract

½ teaspoon kosher salt, plus more to taste

½ cup semi-sweet chocolate chips

Dash of hazelnut extract (optional)

Preheat the oven to 315 degrees F and place hazelnuts on a baking sheet.

Toast the hazelnuts for 5 to 7 minutes, or until they become fragrant and are lightly toasted.

Remove from the oven and let the nuts cool completely.

Add the hazelnuts to a high-powered food processor or blender and blend until they turn into a paste, 6 to 8 minutes. Add the oil about halfway through the process. You may have to stop to scrape down the sides of the container a few times. It might not look like it's going to work, but just keep blending!

Add the cocoa powder, vanilla, and salt and blend until thoroughly mixed and you can no longer see specks of hazelnuts. At this point, the mixture should look fairly homogeneous.

Melt the chocolate chips in a microwave-safe bowl in 30 second increments, stirring after each session, until melted (about three rounds in the microwave).

Add the melted chocolate and blend again until you get a smooth, spreadable texture. If it's still too thick, add a little more oil or just keep blending.

Store in a sealed container in the fridge for up to two weeks. It won't go bad after two weeks; it will just dry out and become less spreadable. Still delicious though.

SAUCES AND SPREADS 69

# QUICK BITES

Never stop eating—aside from skiing as much powder as possible, that's essentially the primary goal during the winter. While some casual outings lend themselves to long breaks and big meals, more often than not, we're constantly snacking on small bites—trying to keep that fire burning all winter long. The recipes in this chapter are the bread and butter of *Ski Snacks* and what initially inspired this book.

In this chapter you'll find easy, everyday snacks, with a variety of flavors that hopefully feel more exciting than your standard granola bar. We've never been more motivated to snack than on days when we have a pack filled with Bacon and Date Rice Bars. In fact, we once ate an entire 8-by-8 tray of them between the two of us on a single ski tour. Truth is, we felt amazing, if not a little uncomfortably full. Candied Spiced Nuts are perfect for snacking while we walk, and Cheesy Polenta Bars are our favorite way to introduce new friends to the wonders of savory snacks.

If you like the food you packed, you're more likely to stop and eat. And the more often you stop and eat, the better you'll feel throughout the day.

Opposite: *We take the charcuterie spread seriously here in the Tetons.*

# ENERGY BALLS, FIVE WAYS

The perfect pick-me-up along the skintrack, date-based energy balls are some of our favorite snacks for a long day out. Sometimes an entire granola bar is more than we want for a quick stop, and eating a small bite like this every thirty minutes to an hour can do wonders for our energy levels throughout a big ski tour. Since we eat so many of these, we like to switch up the flavor combos to keep things interesting. Our first iteration—double-shot mocha—will always be the favorite, but chocolate chip cookie dough is easily a close second. As long as you have the basics covered, feel free to experiment with other nuts, dried fruit, and fillings. These recipes are very substitution friendly, and they look a little different each time.

Store them in the freezer and pluck them out by the handful before heading out for the day.

**Makes 15 to 18 balls**

### FOR THE BASE

1 cup pitted medjool dates

¼ cup rolled oats

1 tablespoon maple syrup, plus more as needed

½ teaspoon vanilla extract

¼ teaspoon kosher salt

### DOUBLE-SHOT MOCHA

¼ cup cocoa powder

¼ cup walnuts

2 tablespoons almond butter

2 tablespoons cacao nibs

2 teaspoons instant espresso powder

Add the base ingredients plus your chosen flavor combo (omitting any toppings or add-ins) to a food processor and blend on high until there are only a few chunks left, about 30 seconds. You may have to stop and scrape the sides down. The mixture should stick together in your fingers. If it's too crumbly, add a tablespoon of water or a dash of maple syrup and blend again.

Transfer the base to a large mixing bowl and mix in any add-ins with your hands.

Use your hands to roll the dough into balls, about 2 tablespoons each, and place on a plate or baking sheet. (For the snickerdoodle version, mix the cinnamon and coconut sugar together in a small bowl and roll each ball in the mixture.) Put the balls in the freezer for at least 1 hour.

## CHOCOLATE CHIP COOKIE DOUGH

¼ cup almonds

2 tablespoons cashew butter

2 tablespoons chocolate chips/chunks (add-ins)

Sprinkle of flake salt (add-ins)

## PEANUT BUTTER COCONUT

¼ cup almonds

¼ cup unsweetened coconut flakes

2 tablespoons peanut butter

## HONEY PISTACHIO

¼ cup toasted pistachios

2 tablespoons cashew butter

1 tablespoon honey

## SNICKERDOODLE

¼ cup cashews

2 tablespoons almond butter

2 tablespoons coconut sugar (topping)

2 teaspoons ground cinnamon (topping)

Once frozen, transfer them to a sealed container so you can reach into the freezer and pluck them out before your next adventure. The frozen balls keep for two to three months.

# LEARNING TO FUEL FROM MY MOM

Most of what I (Lily) have learned about how to fuel for adventures in the mountains comes from my mom. She's been an athlete her whole life—a collegiate swimmer, Ironman triathlete, endurance coach—but in the last few decades, she's translated all of that training and knowledge about fueling into pursuits in the mountains.

I grew up skiing with my family in the Cascades, spending weekends at Crystal Mountain and night skiing at Snoqualmie Pass. When I was in high school, my mom and I discovered backcountry skiing and got hooked pretty quickly. For her, spending long hours climbing uphill on skis was a natural progression from the hours and hours she'd spent racing triathlon. For me, an out-of-shape high school kid with an adventurous attitude but no clue how to pace myself, backcountry skiing hurt in those first few years.

We made a lot of mistakes messing around in the mountains early on—getting lost, scared, and almost benighted. We got stuck on steep kick turns, boot packed in the skintrack, bonked (me), and cried (also me). The saving grace was that my mom knows how to take care of herself. Over the past decade, I've slowly tried to absorb her methods and apply them to my own adventures.

My mom has an impressive engine. She starts slow, warms up, and stops frequently to eat. She frequently feels the best on hour eight of a big tour, and we all consider her a bit of a sandbagger since she's so humble about her strength. She's truly a master at keeping a steady pace—until the last lap, when she's ready to close the gap and signpost you. But most importantly, she knows how to fuel herself for long hours on the skintrack.

She's regimented about getting calories in even when she's not hungry, starting the day with a big meal and never letting up on small, easily digestible snacks (like Butter Mochi). And she always brings enough to share! (See "Bribe Your Friends" sidebar.)

Watching her take the time to train and fuel for long days in the mountains reminds me that it's a long game, and if we take care of ourselves well, we've got decades and decades of winter adventures in the mountains to come.

*Lily and her mom, Cynthia, at the Peter Estin Hut, before a Colorado backcountry ski tour.*

# BACON AND DATE RICE BARS

This recipe is inspired by one of our favorite cookbooks, Biju Thomas and Allen Lim's *Feed Zone Portables*, which got us hooked on homemade rice-based fuel. Filling and easy to digest on the go, rice is a fantastic skintrack snack. This even more so when it's studded with dates and bacon bits, offering the perfect balance of sweet and salty—a real palate pleaser. Because the bars rely on the stickiness of the rice to stay together, they don't last more than a few days in the fridge because the rice starts to dry out and crumble. It's important to use calrose or sushi rice for this recipe as other types of rice, like basmati and jasmine, are not sticky enough. We like to make a big batch before a long weekend and wrap up extras to share with friends.

**Makes 16 bars**

3 cups calrose or sushi rice

4 cups water

1 teaspoon kosher salt, plus more for seasoning

8 ounces bacon, finely chopped

8 to 10 pitted dates (any kind), finely chopped

3 eggs (optional)

Add the rice, water, and salt to a medium saucepan and bring to a boil. Lower the heat, cover, and simmer for 10 to 12 minutes. (Alternatively, combine the rice with 4 cups water in a pressure cooker and cook using normal settings for white rice.)

Grease an 8-by-8-inch pan with cooking spray and set aside.

Heat a small skillet over medium heat and add the bacon.

After the grease from the bacon starts to collect in the bottom of the pan, add the dates and cook until everything is browned, about 5 minutes. If the bacon produces a lot of fat, drain and reserve the excess, leaving about 1 tablespoon in the pan to cook the eggs.

Make a well in the ingredients in the center of the skillet and crack the eggs into the well.

Scramble the eggs and stir everything together.

Once the rice is cooked, place it in a large bowl with the bacon, dates, and eggs. Stir well.

Add salt to taste before pressing the contents into an 8-by-8-inch pan and placing it in the fridge for at least 1 hour.

When the bars are cool, cut them into 16 squares and wrap them in foil immediately. Store bars in the fridge for up to five days.

# CHEESY POLENTA BARS

We love chocolate and peanut butter as much as the next skier, but sometimes sweet treats just don't hit the spot. When we're in the mood for something savory, we turn to a big batch of these cheesy polenta bars. These are one of the simplest snacks to make, and yet they somehow garner the most surprise when we whip one out on the trail. Polenta? In the backcountry? Why not? Serve them to your Southern transplant friends who want a comforting taste of grits in the snowy hills of the Rockies. Note: these aren't the sturdiest bars out there, so wrap them in something that seals (like a reusable Stasher bag or well-loved resealable plastic bags).

**Makes 16 bars**

3 cups water

¾ teaspoon kosher salt

1 cup polenta

Add the water and salt to a saucepan and bring to a boil.

Grease an 8-by-8-inch baking pan with butter or coconut oil.

¼ cup grated sharp
cheddar cheese

¼ cup crumbled
goat cheese

¼ cup finely chopped
chives or green onions

¼ cup chopped cooked
bacon (optional)

Once the water is boiling, add the polenta and cook over medium heat, stirring constantly to get rid of any big clumps.

Once the polenta starts to thicken (about 5 minutes), add the cheddar cheese, goat cheese, chives, and bacon (if using).

Remove from the heat and stir for another 2 to 3 minutes. Taste and add more salt if needed.

Pour the polenta into the baking pan and let cool on the counter until it reaches room temperature. Cover and refrigerate for at least 1 hour before cutting into bars. The bars will keep in the fridge for up to five days.

## DELICIOUS AND NUTRITIONIST-APPROVED SNACKS

### KAYLEE PICKETT

Cheesy polenta bars are a great example of a simple savory snack that is easy to pack and has a bit of everything you need on the trail: simple sugars, protein, fat, and salt. Polenta is a simple carbohydrate so it will digest easily and quickly. A single bar provides 333 calories, 18 grams of protein, and 24 grams of fat to fuel you up and supply long-lasting energy that will sustain your efforts for over an hour. Salt from the bacon and butter helps maintain fluid balance and hydration. Calcium and potassium help your muscles contract so you can keep moving uphill.

# OATMEAL BANANA COOKIES, THREE WAYS

Admittedly, these are probably some of the least photogenic trail snacks we've made, but don't write them off because they look like mush. It's basically a bowl of oatmeal in a portable, cookie shape, which is ideal for groggy mornings when you just can't get much breakfast down before hopping in the car. Lily usually pops three or four of these in her jacket pocket and eats them within the first hour of skinning, as a second breakfast. The fun part about them is that, like many of our variation-friendly snacks, they look a little different each time. These are three of our favorite flavor combos, but feel free to scour the pantry for other fun add-ins—like nuts, seeds, sturdy fruits and veggies, candy . . . most ingredients taste best when served in cookie form.

**Makes 12 to 18 cookies**

### FOR THE BASE

2 to 3 medium-sized, ripe bananas (about 2 cups mashed)

1 cup oat flour

½ cup rolled oats

½ teaspoon vanilla extract

¼ teaspoon kosher salt

### BERRY CHOCOLATE CHIP

⅓ cup dark chocolate chips or chunks

⅓ cup walnut pieces

½ cup raspberries, blackberries, or chopped strawberries

Preheat the oven to 350 degrees F and line a baking sheet with parchment paper.

Mash the bananas with a fork or masher in a medium bowl.

Add the oat flour and stir well.

Add the oats, vanilla, and salt, and stir again.

Mix in the ingredients from your flavor of choice. (If you're including berries, wait until the very last minute to stir them in so they don't break apart.)

Let the dough sit on the counter or in the fridge for at least 15 minutes so the oats can hydrate.

Use a spoon to scoop the dough onto your baking sheet, 1 generous spoonful (or 1 heaping tablespoon) per cookie. The dough won't spread

## CINNAMON APPLE DATE

½ cup finely chopped apple (about half of a medium apple)

⅓ cup finely chopped dried dates

⅓ cup walnut pieces

½ teaspoon ground cinnamon

½ teaspoon ground nutmeg

## CARROT ZUCCHINI PECAN

½ cup finely shredded carrot

⅓ cup pecans

⅓ cup raisins or dried cherries

¼ cup finely shredded zucchini

out, so you can line the cookies up really close together. If you prefer a larger or smaller cookie, you may need to adjust the baking time.

Bake for 11 to 13 minutes, or until the dough is no longer mushy and golden brown. Let cool.

Store in a sealed container in the fridge for up to one week.

# JAMMY BANANA THUMBPRINTS

A level up from our classic Oatmeal Banana Cookies, these super easy thumbprints are just another way to enjoy homemade quick jam, our favorite way to preserve the summer's bounty for the darkest winter days. These cookies require a little more care while transporting compared to our standard banana cookies. Ideally, they should be transported in a sealed, hard-sided container to avoid spreading jam all over the inside of your backpack or pocket. Feel free to swap out the walnuts and pumpkin seeds for your preferred nuts and seeds.

**Makes 14 to 16 cookies**

2 to 3 medium ripe
bananas (about 2
cups mashed)

1 cup oat flour

½ cup plain instant
oatmeal
(or quick-cooking oats)

½ cup mixture of chopped
walnuts and pumpkin
seeds

1 tablespoon chia seeds

½ teaspoon ground
cinnamon

½ teaspoon vanilla extract

¼ teaspoon kosher salt

½ cup homemade
jam, such as Quick
Plum Rhubarb Jam, or
store-bought

Preheat the oven to 350 degrees F and line a baking sheet with parchment paper.

Mash the bananas with a fork or masher in a medium bowl.

Add oat flour and stir well.

Add the oatmeal mix, walnuts and pumpkin seeds, chia seeds, cinnamon, vanilla, and salt, and stir until everything is well mixed.

Let the dough sit on the counter or in the fridge for at least 15 minutes so the oats can hydrate.

Use a spoon to scoop the dough onto the baking sheet, about 2 tablespoons (or 1 very generous spoonful) per cookie. The cookies won't spread at all, so don't worry too much about spacing.

Using your thumb, make a deep imprint in the center of each cookie.

Fill the imprint with a generous dollop of jam.

Bake for 11 to 13 minutes, or until the cookies are all firmed up. Let cool.

Store in a sealed container in the fridge for up to one week.

# ANTS ON A DATE

This recipe came to us from Sarah Duggan, who likes to get her hands dirty; we often find her kneading dough in her kitchen, shaping clay on a potter's wheel, or zooming through the dirt on her mountain bike. She also works with a local nonprofit to create a stronger community in Jackson, Wyoming.

Sarah says, "I have a sweet tooth, especially when my body is working hard in the mountains. I often fill my snack bag with Sour Patch Kids or a Snickers bar to satisfy that craving, but when I have time to prepare my own treats, this recipe is a staple. My college roommate introduced me to this idea years ago, and it's been a special treat on many backcountry adventures since. I make a big batch and keep them in the fridge. Pull them out at the last minute in the summertime so they don't get too gooey. In the winter, they survive well in the frigid temps (unlike me)!"

This is a fun recipe to make with kids; they'll love making them and eating them, a delicious way to start sharing the love of homemade snacking at a young age.

**Makes 12 dates**

12 medjool dates with pits

¼ cup peanut butter

Handful of mini chocolate chips

Slice open each date lengthwise and remove the pit.

Spoon about a teaspoon of peanut butter into each date.

Sprinkle a few mini chocolate chips on top of the peanut butter.

Store in a sealed container in the fridge until ready to eat or pack up. If you stack the dates, place parchment paper between each layer to prevent them from sticking. Eat within two weeks.

 **SKID HACK:** If you want to go ultra-skid, skip the peanut butter and chocolate altogether and snack on plain, pitted dates. It's the perfect sweet bite for a quick midstride pick-me-up with zero prep.

# POCKET QUICHE, TWO WAYS

We love to push the boundaries of "portable" food. Yes, we agree that quiche is best served warm, eaten with a fork, and savored while staring up at the snowcapped peaks of Chamonix. But it also makes a darn good ski snack (so long as you don't smoosh it into oblivion), to be enjoyed while kicking back on your favorite summit. We recreated two *classique* quiches in bite-sized form, so we can take a little piece of our favorite French breakfast with us wherever we go: Quiche épinard, because we can always use a little more green in our diet. (Tossing spinach in with lots of cheese counts, right?) And quiche lorraine, because we can't think of anything better than bacon, cheese, eggs, and puff pastry for a pick-me-up in the mountains.

**Makes 12 mini quiches**

## FOR THE BASE

1 sheet frozen
puff pastry

5 eggs

½ cup milk (non-dairy
works too, as long as it's
unsweetened)

½ teaspoon kosher salt

½ teaspoon black pepper

## QUICHE ÉPINARD

1 cup chopped fresh
spinach

½ cup goat cheese

## QUICHE
## LORRAINE

4 slices bacon, cooked
and chopped

⅓ cup gruyère cheese

Take the puff pastry out of the fridge and let thaw on the counter for 15 to 20 minutes, until malleable but not sticky.

Preheat the oven to 400 degrees F and grease a 12-cup muffin pan with cooking spray.

Roll out the puff pastry until it's about half as thin as it was when it was frozen. Cut into 12 even squares, and line each muffin cup with a piece of puff pastry.

Add the eggs to a large bowl and whisk well.

Stir in the milk and salt. Then add your filling of choice.

Divide the egg mixture evenly between the 12 cups. Sprinkle with the black pepper and bake for 12 to 15 minutes, until a knife inserted in the center comes out clean.

Let cool and store in an airtight container in the fridge for up to one week, or in the freezer for up to one month.

QUICK BITES 87

# BACON-WRAPPED DATES WITH GOAT CHEESE

Sweet-and-salty snacks are what keep us coming back for more. Bacon-wrapped dates are one of our favorite crowd-pleasing appetizers to take to dinner parties (simple, addictive, and easy to make a lot of). And you'll see, as we quickly discovered, they taste just as delicious the next day. Here we elevate standard bacon-wrapped dates by stuffing them with goat cheese for a truly indulgent snack.

We usually go a little lighter on the bacon, by cutting the pieces pretty thin, so it doesn't overpower the date and goat cheese. But if you're all about the bacon, and the dates and goat cheese are really just a delivery mechanism, feel free to double the bacon.

**Makes 20 dates**

20 pitted medjool dates

4 ounces goat cheese

5 slices thin-cut bacon, cut in half and lengthwise

Preheat the oven to 410 degrees F and line a baking sheet with parchment paper.

With a paring knife, slice open each date lengthwise.

Fill each date with 1 heaping teaspoon of goat cheese.

Wrap a thin slice of bacon as tightly as you can around each date and place it on the baking sheet. Use toothpicks if you're having a hard time getting everything to stick together.

Bake for 6 minutes, then flip and bake for 6 more. You may need a few extra minutes in the oven, but check them frequently since they can burn quickly.

Let cool and store in a sealed container in the fridge for up to one week.

# CHOCOLATE-DIPPED POCKET BACON

We love chocolate, and we love bacon. So why not mix together two of the greatest food groups? When shared, this is the kind of snack that turns casual acquaintances into lifelong friends. To take these treats on the trail, be sure to stash them in a sealed bag to prevent pocket chocolate, which sounds way better than it actually is.

**Makes 8 to 10 pieces**

1 pound thick-cut bacon

2 teaspoons coconut oil

6 ounces semisweet or dark chocolate

Flake salt, for finishing

Heat a large cast iron skillet over medium-high heat.

Add the bacon slices in batches, cooking about 3 to 5 minutes on each side until brown and slightly crispy.

Prepare a plate with a few paper towels, and transfer the cooked bacon to the plate.

Let the bacon cool for 15 to 20 minutes.

Melt the chocolate and coconut oil in the microwave, stirring every 30 seconds, or use a double boiler to melt the chocolate.

Prepare a small baking sheet or second plate with parchment paper.

Dip each piece of bacon in the chocolate, coating half the slice, and let the excess drip off. Then place each slice on the parchment paper. Repeat until you've dipped each slice. We prefer to coat half the bacon for a less messy prepping and eating experience, but feel free to use a fork and dunk the slices all the way in, if you want.

Sprinkle the chocolate with flake salt and place the tray or plate in the fridge for at least 1 hour (or 15 minutes in the freezer if you're in a hurry!) to chill the chocolate.

Keep in a sealed container in the fridge for up to one week.

## MOTIVATED BY FOOD

### NICOLE JORGENSEN

Food in the mountains is such an important part of the adventure. I like to have my easy snacks like gummies handy for fuel that doesn't require stopping, but I also like to use my bigger and more creative snacks and meals as motivation on big days. I'm a huge fan of saving my sandwich for the summit or a perch with good views! Also, packing food with a variety of tastes keeps me interested and fueled. I enjoy gummy candy, baked goods, a pastry, or a good old classic meat and cheese sandwich. For days that are more about the food than the mission, I love a good charcute-ski or backcountry fondue.

*Nicole Jorgensen is a ski patroller, emergency-room nurse, and mountain adventurer living in Ketchum, Idaho. She loves exploring on skis or anything with two wheels.*

# CRISPY NUT BUTTER BARS

These crunchy bars entered our repertoire a few years ago, when Lily wanted to see if she could go an entire winter without eating anything from a wrapper while skiing. It was one of our first forays into homemade ski snacks, and she baked up a storm and learned a lot about batching recipes and freezing treats. These bars quickly became one of our go-to snacks. We frequently double the batch, cut them into bars, wrap, and freeze them, so all we have to do is open the freezer, pluck out two at a time, and head out the door. And yes, so many store-bought granola bars are peanut butter or chocolate flavored . . . but this homemade version is truly delicious!

**Makes 16 bars**

## FOR THE BARS

1 ½ cups rolled oats

1 cup brown rice crisps or rice cereal (see Skid Hack)

¼ cup almond flour

¼ cup ground flax seeds

¾ teaspoon kosher salt

¾ cup creamy peanut butter, or nut butter of choice

⅓ cup honey

2 teaspoons coconut oil

1 teaspoon vanilla extract

Line an 8-by-8-inch baking pan with parchment paper, leaving a bit hanging over two sides of the pan to allow for easy removal.

In a large bowl, mix together the oats, rice crisps, almond flour, flax seeds, and kosher salt. Set aside.

In a small saucepan (or in the microwave), melt the nut butter, honey, coconut oil, and vanilla on low heat until you can stir it evenly.

Pour the nut butter mixture over the dry ingredients and mix well with a spoon.

The mixture should stick together but be moist enough that you can press it into a pan. If it's too thick, add 1 tablespoon of nut butter at a time. If it's too thin, add a handful of oats.

Press the mixture tightly into the baking pan and place it in the freezer while you melt the chocolate. The tighter you pack the mixture, the better shape your granola bars will hold.

## FOR THE CHOCOLATE TOPPING

½ to ¾ cup dark chocolate chips (use ¾ cup if you like a thicker chocolate layer!)

2 teaspoons coconut oil

Flake salt, to top

Add the chocolate chips and coconut oil to a small, microwave-safe bowl and microwave for 30-second increments on low for a few rounds until melted. Stir between each round.

Remove the bars from the freezer and pour the chocolate mixture over the top, sprinkle with flake salt, and place in the fridge for at least 30 minutes.

Once chilled, lift the parchment paper out of the baking pan and place the square of granola on a cutting board to cut into bars.

The bars can be kept in the fridge for up to two weeks or frozen for up to two months.

**SKID HACK:** For chocolate lovers (hand raise!) stir in cocoa rice cereal instead of plain for an extra indulgent bite.

# MADS BALLS

These nutrient-dense balls made with nuts, figs, and chocolate are named for professional skier Madison Ostergren, who introduced us to the recipe. Lily took a ski guiding course with her in the Tetons in January of 2024, and much to her delight, Mads brought plenty of delicious snacks for early morning ski tours. "You *have* to try Mads Balls," Mads exclaimed early one morning in the car, immediately passing over a handful of these portable treats. We've become accustomed to offering snacks to our friends while skiing, so it was a welcome surprise to enjoy a new creation from a new friend! According to Mads, these snacks are "the perfect ski touring snack because they are sweet and salty and have delicious ingredients that make you feel good when you eat them."

We can't claim to make them exactly how Mads does (we often run out of some nut or seed), so while our rendition has become a little less precise, we do our best to recreate this energizing snack!

An ex-ski racer turned freeride mountaineer, Mads loves skiing technical lines, climbing, mountain running, and playing guitar and ukulele with her friends. She's often skiing or climbing in Grand Teton National Park or dancing until she drops.

---

**Makes 30 to 35 balls**

1 cup dried figs

½ cup walnuts

½ cup pecans

½ cup cashews

1 ½ cups oats

½ cup pepitas (pumpkin seeds)

½ cup chia seeds

½ cup flax meal

In a food processor, pulse together the figs, walnuts, pecans, and cashews until it becomes a coarse mixture.

Mix in the oats and pepitas and pulse again, about 20 seconds; the mixture will be coarse. Transfer the blended mixture to a large bowl.

Stir in the chia seeds, flax meal, collagen peptides or cocoa powder, and sea salt.

In a medium bowl, stir together the coconut oil, almond butter, honey, and maple syrup. Add this

2 to 3 servings of chocolate collagen peptides, or ¼ cup cocoa powder

Sprinkle of sea salt

¾ cup melted coconut oil

¾ cup almond butter

¼ cup honey

¼ cup maple syrup

⅓ cup semisweet or dark chocolate chips

to the nut mixture and stir until well combined. Stir in the chocolate chips.

The mixture should hold when pressed together. If it's too wet, add more nuts or oats; if it's too crumbly, add more honey or almond butter. Scoop out about 2 tablespoons at a time and roll into balls.

Place balls on a baking sheet and freeze for at least 1 hour, then transfer to a sealed storage container. Store in the freezer for up to one month and grab a few as you head out on your next adventure!

*(Photo by Madison Ostergren)*

# APPLE-BRIE PROSCIUTTO ROLL-UPS

On long days and overnight trips in the mountains, Lily always misses fresh fruit. She'll occasionally toss an apple in her bag, but it can be hard to justify the weight (or find time to eat it!). In these roll-ups, crunchy sliced apples are enhanced by the salty goodness of prosciutto and a thin slice of creamy brie cheese. We use Pink Lady apples (Lily's favorite) because we love the contrast of tartness paired with salty prosciutto, but feel free to use your apple of choice.

**Makes 16 roll-ups**

1 large apple

4 ounces brie cheese

8 slices prosciutto, halved lengthwise

Slice the apple and brie into similar-sized pieces.

Stack one slice of apple and one slice of brie and wrap each stack with a half slice of prosciutto.

Store in an airtight container in the fridge for up to four days.

# ONIGIRI, THREE WAYS

A pilgrimage to Japan is essential for any powder-loving skier. And while the dreamy powder skiing certainly delivers, it's the food that makes a ski trip to Japan one to remember. If you've talked to anyone who's skied in Japan, you've likely heard about the impressive selection of high-quality snacks you'll find at 7-Eleven (a locale you couldn't pay us to eat at in the US), including a variety of onigiri. Each day, we ate no fewer than five of these delicious rice balls stuffed with fish, veggies, or meat and wrapped with nori. We snacked on onigiri on chairlifts, summits, and bullet train rides back to Tokyo.

Making these by hand is very doable, but it's even easier with an onigiri mold (easy to find online). Ours is a little triangular onigiri mold we picked up in Tokyo. If you make them by hand, be sure to keep your hands wet to prevent the rice from sticking to your fingers. Like all rice-based treats, these are best eaten fairly fresh. Make them in small batches and eat within a day or two. If you're really craving some extra salt in the mountains, pack a little grocery-store packet of soy sauce to pour on them.

---

**Makes 6 to 8 onigiri**

### FOR THE BASE

1 cup sushi or calrose rice

1 ¾ cups water

¼ cup rice vinegar

1 tablespoon white sugar

1 teaspoon kosher salt

1 10-by-10-inch nori sheet, cut into 1-inch strips

To prepare the rice, rinse the rice in a strainer under cold running water for 1 minute. Let air dry for 8 to 10 minutes.

Combine the rice and water in a large saucepan and set over high heat.

Bring to a boil, then immediately turn down heat and simmer. Cover and cook for 15 to 20 minutes, until the rice is soft. (Alternatively, combine the rice with 1 ¼ cups water in a pressure cooker or Instant Pot and cook using normal settings for white rice.)

In a small bowl, whisk together the vinegar, sugar, and salt to make seasoning.

## CLASSIC TUNA MAYO

2 (5-ounce) cans tuna in olive oil

½ cup Kewpie mayo

2 teaspoons kosher salt

Togarashi spice, for topping

## MISO VEGGIE

6 tablespoons miso paste

4 tablespoons water

¾ cup finely chopped raw veggies of choice (green onion, carrots, or even kale!)

Sesame seeds, for topping

Pour seasoning over rice. Mix well.

Let cool for 20 to 30 minutes before shaping.

Meanwhile, prepare your chosen filling (instructions follow).

With wet hands, form rice balls that are 2 to 3 inches in diameter. Make a well in the center of each rice ball and fill it with 2 tablespoons of filling, then close up the rice around the filling.

Wrap each rice ball with 1 strip of nori and sprinkle with togarashi or sesame seeds.

*Continues on next page*

## BBQ BEEF

½ cup brown sugar

¼ cup soy sauce

1 tablespoon sesame oil

2 cloves garlic, minced

1 teaspoon freshly grated ginger

1 pound ground beef

Togarashi spice, for topping

## CLASSIC TUNA MAYO

Combine the tuna, mayo, and salt in a small bowl and mix thoroughly.

## MISO VEGGIE

Stir the miso paste and water together in a small bowl.

Toss the veggies into the bowl and coat with miso.

## BBQ BEEF

Combine the brown sugar, soy sauce, sesame oil, garlic, and ginger in a small bowl.

Put the ground beef in a medium bowl and pour the marinade over the top. Place in the fridge for 10 to 15 minutes.

Heat a medium skillet over medium heat and toss in the marinated beef. Cook for 10 minutes, stirring occasionally.

Remove the beef from the skillet and let cool on plate.

# SPAM MUSUBI

This snack is, perhaps, the only modern-day consumption of SPAM we'll advocate for. We discovered the delicious world of SPAM musubi while visiting Lily's aunt Chris in Hawaii a few years back. This popular Hawaiian snack, made up of white rice, nori, and pan-fried slices of SPAM, dates back to World War II. You'll find it at tons of small markets and corner stores throughout the islands. Sitting on the beach in flip-flops, we each took one bite and immediately exclaimed, "What a perfect ski snack!"

---

**Makes 6 to 8 musubi**

½ cup light soy sauce

¼ cup brown sugar

1 (12-ounce) can SPAM, sliced into ¼-inch-thick pieces

3 cups cooked sushi or calrose rice (see Onigiri recipe for cooking instructions)

1 sheet nori, cut into 1-inch strips

Preheat a skillet on medium heat.

Combine the soy sauce and brown sugar in a small bowl.

Dip the SPAM slices into the sauce, then fry in the skillet for 6 to 8 minutes, turning once. Remove from the heat.

Form rectangular rice blocks (1-inch thick, 2-to-3-inches long) and place a fried SPAM slice on each block.

Wrap each block in a strip of nori.

QUICK BITES

# QUICK CANDIED SPICED NUTS, FOUR WAYS

We love sugar. And luckily, our bodies tend to need a whole lot of it on the skintrack. Candied nuts are a quick way to pack in much-needed calories while out in the snow, plus they're just so darn tasty that we started throwing them on salads and snacking on them for an afternoon pick-me-up. They come together quickly, even given the time it takes to roast the nuts (it's worth it!), and the recipe is easy to customize to whatever nut or spice you want. Start with 2 cups of nuts, ½ cup sugar, and ¼ teaspoon salt, then add your choice of spices. These are a few of our favorites.

## CINNAMON SUGAR ALMONDS

2 cups raw almonds

½ cup sugar

¼ teaspoon kosher salt

½ teaspoon ground cinnamon

Flake salt, for topping

## SWEET AND SPICY WALNUTS

2 cups raw walnuts

½ cup sugar

¼ teaspoon kosher salt

½ teaspoon ground cayenne pepper

Flake salt, for topping

Preheat oven to 350 degrees F.

Spread the nuts on a baking sheet and toast for 5 to 7 minutes, until fragrant and starting to brown. Remove and set aside. Prepare the coating.

Heat the sugar in a wide saucepan over medium heat. Add the salt and spices (except the flake salt) and stir until it all melts together. The candy coating will firm up quickly, within about 20 seconds, so stir it all together immediately.

Remove from heat, add the nuts, and stir until everything is coated. Line the baking sheet with parchment paper and spread the nuts across the baking sheet.

Sprinkle with flake salt, if desired. Let cool for 15 minutes and enjoy!

*Continues on next page*

## SALTED COCOA PECANS

2 cups raw pecans

½ cup sugar

¼ teaspoon kosher salt

2 teaspoons cocoa powder

Flake salt, for topping

## TURMERIC GINGER CASHEWS

2 cups raw cashews

½ cup sugar

¼ teaspoon kosher salt

½ teaspoon ground turmeric

½ teaspoon ground ginger

½ teaspoon ground cinnamon

Flake salt, for topping

# A MOUNTAIN RUNNER'S CAUTIONARY TALE

### TAYLOR FRY

Sure, I could have trained more than doing just one 20-plus mile run before running the 40-mile Teton Crest Trail (TCT), but hey, people have done more with way less. Still, it was a gratifying journey of torment, joy, and my first major bonk due to improper fueling. Halfway through, I felt my body starting to shut down. Turns out googling "what to eat during a long run" the night before didn't give me clear-cut answers on what would help me best push my body to its limits.

What I craved was absolutely nothing I brought. My vest had bars, something I had baked that ended up more cake-like than intended, and a ton of water. The only thing I wanted? Salt. I craved it like I was pregnant with Poseidon's baby. Thankfully, a seasoned distance runner and friend brought a small water bottle of bloody mary mix, electrolyte tabs (pop those straight into your mouth if desperate), and pickle juice.

After finishing the run, I went into a rabbit hole of what makes the best running fuel. I had visions of returning to the TCT with salt-lined pockets and a taste for redemption. So far, the anti-bonk trail fuel list includes onigiri, pickle packs, bloody mary mix, and my favorite salty electrolyte mix. Learn from my mistakes!

*Taylor Fry is a writer and photographer based in Wilson, Wyoming. Drawn to small and tall tales, she bounds between mountain ranges and coastlines, taking inspiration from the in-betweens and nothing-at-alls.*

# SCHNITZEL STRIPS

Like many of our recipes, this one came to us by accident after getting back from a long ski tour and gorging ourselves on leftovers from the fridge. The night before, we had made lots of schnitzel and somehow hadn't finished it—our future selves were quite happy about that one. We cut it into strips and ate it like Austrian chicken tenders, dipped in mustard and sweet jam. On the trail, this delicious savory snack transports quite well in a small plastic sandwich bag. If you're feeling like you need condiments, pack a few fast-food packs of your favorite sauces, and your friends will look on in awe as you dip away.

**Makes 10 to 12 strips**

2 thin, 8-to-10-ounce boneless pork chops or chicken breasts

1 cup vegetable oil (for frying)

Use a meat tenderizer (or anything heavy covered in plastic wrap—we've used the heel of a ski boot in a pinch) to pound the pork chops until they are ¼-inch thick.

½ cup polenta

1 tablespoon kosher salt

1 tablespoon ground black pepper

1 tablespoon finely chopped fresh herbs, such as oregano and rosemary

2 eggs

Heat the oil in a large skillet over medium-high heat.

On a large plate, mix the polenta, salt, pepper, and herbs.

Crack the eggs into a small bowl and whisk lightly.

Dip each tenderized pork chop into the egg, then toss it into the polenta mixture and turn to coat.

Transfer the pork chops to the skillet and fry for 5 to 6 minutes on each side, until golden brown.

Remove from the pan and let drain on a paper towel.

Once cool enough to handle, cut the schnitzels into ¾-inch strips and store in a sealed container in the fridge, for up to one week, until ready to eat or pack.

**SKID HACK:** Sometimes we do our best and it's not quite enough. On those days, it's all right that the "recipe" looks like this:

1 late shift at work

1 missed alarm clock

$2.50, cash or card

1 to 2 overly ambitious ski partners

Sprint out of your house in a panic with skis in tow.

Stop by your nearest 24-hour gas station. Purchase as many Snickers bars as possible.

QUICK BITES 109

# SUMMIT SANDWICHES

When do you prefer to eat your best snacks? Do you save your favorite treat for the summit, or eat it immediately? Scarf down the whole thing as soon as the craving strikes? Save half for the bushwhack on the exit? Max has been known to eat his favorite summit sandwiches within an hour of leaving the trailhead to "lighten the load" on the way up the mountain.

Since sandwiches are almost always best enjoyed fresh, most of these recipes make just one sandwich, but we encourage you to make extra filling to stash in the fridge for fresh sandos on the daily. Our Smashed Chickpea and Avocado Sandwich filling keeps well for up to one week in the fridge, rewarding planners who want to be ready when sandwich cravings strike (it's also great as a dip with crackers). And we can never get enough olive tapenade, so be sure to make extra when whipping up a Brooklyn Italian.

And though these sandwiches may be designed to be eaten on the summit, we hereby give you permission to eat them whenever you damn well please. And if you want to really step it up a notch, throw that all out the window and just make two!

*Opposite: Indulging in a skintrack baguette in Chamonix, France—*
*the birthplace of many of our Summit Sandwiches*

# PESTO, EGG, AND AVOCADO SANDWICH

Breakfast sandwiches are absolutely not reserved for the morning, but often when we get an alpine start (out the door well before dawn), we're on the summit not long after breakfast time. So why not enjoy a pesto-filled egg sandwich while you rip your skins? We've definitely had our fair share of breakfast sandwiches that get mushy, make a huge mess in your bag, and just aren't actually all that good after they've been in your bag all morning, so we designed this recipe specifically with portability in mind.

**Makes 1 sandwich**

1 whole wheat english muffin

1 teaspoon coconut oil

½ of a small avocado

Sprinkle of flake salt

2 tablespoons Everyday Pesto

1 egg

Sprinkle of ground black pepper

Handful of spinach

1 slice sharp cheddar cheese

Pop your english muffin into the toaster.

Meanwhile, heat the coconut oil in a small skillet over medium-high heat.

Use a fork to smash the avocado on one side of the english muffin, then sprinkle it with flake salt. Spread pesto on the other side of the muffin.

Once the pan is hot, crack the egg into the center and sprinkle it with salt and pepper.

Use a spatula to scramble the egg without spreading it out too much (it should stay roughly the same diameter as when it was cracked into the pan). You may need to use the spatula to keep it together.

Flip the egg after about 90 seconds and let cook for another minute or so, until it is cooked through.

Layer the spinach on the avocado side of the english muffin, then add cheese.

Remove the egg from the pan and place it on top of the cheese. Top with extra salt and pepper, then cover with the pesto side of the muffin.

Let cool for 10 minutes, then wrap it in foil and hit the road!

# TOMATO JAM AND ARUGULA BREAKFAST SAMMIE

There's something about combining tomato jam and goat cheese that's just absolutely irresistible. This breakfast sammie was inspired by a sandwich Lily ordered at one of her all-time favorite cafes: Arête Coffee Bar in North Bend, Washington. It shares a building with a ski shop (dangerous) and serves an incredible array of pastries and breakfast sandwiches all day, the perfect stop before or after a big adventure. Lily says, "I remember chowing down on one of these sandwiches after a long, rainy ski tour on Snoqualmie Pass. It turned a soggy excursion into a delicious memory. And every time I make one of these, I think about how quickly an excellent sandwich can turn a day around." Whip up one of these sammies and head out into a storm. You won't regret it.

**Makes 1 sandwich**

1 tablespoon unsalted butter, plus more for the bread

¼ cup white onion, finely sliced

1 egg

Pinch of kosher salt

2 slices of sourdough bread

1 ounce goat cheese

2 tablespoons tomato jam

Handful of arugula

Add the butter to a nonstick pan and heat to medium.

Add the onion and sauté until it becomes translucent and starts to caramelize, 6 to 8 minutes. Remove the onions from the heat and add a little bit of extra butter to the pan.

Crack the egg into the pan and slightly scramble the yolk while keeping the egg contained. Sprinkle with salt. Flip the egg after about 90 seconds and let it cook for another minute or so, until it's cooked through.

Lightly toast the bread.

Spread butter on both slices of bread, then spread goat cheese on the bottom slice and tomato jam on the top slice.

Place the egg on top of the goat cheese, then top with the onion and arugula. Close the sandwich, slice in half, and wrap up your breakfast to enjoy in the lift line.

# LE CHAMONIARD BAGUETTE

If there's one thing we've learned from our time in Chamonix, it's that there is no such thing as a wrong time for a baguette. In the tram line, waiting to zip up nine-thousand vertical feet into the icy heights of Mont Blanc, it's not uncommon to see both an ice tool and a baguette strapped to the outside of a skier's pack. The best part of this one? It's pretty much the easiest sandwich to make.

**Makes 1 sandwich**

1 (12-inch) baguette

1 tablespoon Classic Aioli

2 teaspoons salted butter

4 ounces roasted ham, sliced

3 ounces emmental cheese, sliced

5 cornichons, sliced in half

Slice the baguette lengthwise, leaving one long edge intact.

Spread aioli on the top half of the baguette, and butter on the bottom.

Layer the ham, then the cheese, and top with cornichons.

Close up your sandwich and stash it in your pack until you reach the top of a steep, harrowing bootpack.

# HOW TO BUILD THE PERFECT SANDWICH

Building the ultimate sandwich might seem like a simple proposition. But let's be real, we've all eaten plenty of things that pass as a "sandwich" that are anything but good. Whether it's sad bread, soggy ingredients, or just the wrong sauce, there are definitely many ways for things to go wrong between the bread. When you eat a truly delicious sandwich, you know it as soon as you take the first bite. So what's the secret?

### Rule 1: Use Good Bread (Duh)

Don't cut corners on bread. This one should go without saying, but the quickest way to ruin a sandwich is by using bread (or whatever vessel you may be using) that's subpar. Ideally it should be fresh, and it should be the right type for the job. We chose specific breads for our recipes for flavor, of course, but also for texture and durability (see Rule 3).

### Rule 2: Learn to Layer

Much like knowing the layering of your local snowpack, the proper layering of ingredients inside your sandwich is a vital piece to the sandwich-making puzzle. It's not just about getting the right flavors—it's also up to you to engineer a structurally sound sandwich. Make sure to layer anything that can slide (sliced meats and cheeses or slippery tomatoes) right next to something sticky (sauce) or coarse, like the bread itself. You don't want the unfortunate experience of a sandwich coming apart mid-bite.

### Rule 3: Balance Flavors and Textures

Contrast is the key to a great sandwich. Sweet apple and savory cheese, crunchy lettuce and soft sourdough bread. We always aim to mix up our textures and flavors to balance things out. Variety is the spice of life!

**Rule 4: To Toast or Not to Toast?**

The answer is that it depends. Certain breads (sourdough, an english muffin, or multigrain, specifically) are delicious when they're lightly toasted. Others, like a baguette, are best enjoyed fresh. (Toasting is a great way to resurrect bread that was left for a few days on the counter.)

**Rule 5: Pack It Securely**

When you're on the go, make sure to wrap your sandwiches tightly. That will keep them intact, prevent any unfortunate spillage, take up less space in your pack, and make your first bite atop that hard-earned summit all the better.

*When you're headed into the backcountry, stash sandwiches at the top of your pack to prevent inadvertent smooshing.*

SUMMIT SANDWICHES

# SMASHED CHICKPEA AND AVOCADO SANDWICH

While we love a good egg salad sandwich, the smell can wreak havoc on the inside of your pack during a long, sunny ski tour. The chickpea smash stuffed inside this hippie-dippie sandwich is hearty and filling, plus the whole sandwich is vegan, for all our plant-based amigos. The filling recipe makes enough for at least four sandwiches. Keep a stash of it in the fridge to make fresh sandwiches on the daily—or eat the smashed chickpea filling with crackers for an afternoon snack.

**Makes 1 sandwich**

## FOR THE CHICKPEA SMASH

1 (15.5-ounce) can chickpeas, rinsed and drained

1 tablespoon vegan mayo (use regular if you prefer)

2 teaspoons fresh lemon juice

2 teaspoons extra-virgin olive oil

½ teaspoon kosher salt

½ teaspoon cracked black pepper

1 celery stalk, finely chopped

1 medium carrot, finely chopped

1 small dill pickle, finely chopped (optional)

## FOR THE SANDWICH

2 slices whole wheat bread

½ avocado

Extra flake salt, to taste

Handful of spinach or lettuce

Handful of sprouts

Add the chickpeas to a medium bowl and mash with a fork until you have a coarse mixture with only a few whole chickpeas left. Don't take out all your anger at missing last week's storm on these poor little beans—we're not aiming for full-on hummus.

Add the lemon juice, olive oil, mayo, salt, and pepper and mash again.

Stir in celery, carrots, and pickle, if using.

Toast both slices of bread.

Use a fork to smash the avocado onto both pieces of bread and sprinkle flake salt on top.

Layer a handful of spinach or lettuce on the bottom slice, then add about ¼ of the chickpea smash. Depending on how many fixings you piled on, you may have a little extra smash, so use your best judgment when deciding how much to add.

Place a handful of sprouts on top, then put a lid on it with the top slice of avocado toast. Slice in half, wrap with foil, and bust it out on top of a snowy peak!

Store the rest of the chickpea smash in a sealed container for up to one week and enjoy with crackers or on tomorrow's sandwich.

# POWDER DAY TURKEY CLUB

An all-time classic. We don't think we're alone when we say that a good turkey club is one of life's simplest pleasures. Sure, you can always get a store-bought one on the way to the mountain (and we'll readily admit that's our empty-fridge-emergency go-to), but a homemade turkey club will have you fending off "can I have a bite" requests from your ski partners the second you pull it out. Plus, after extensive on-slope testing, we've determined that our ski turns are *much* better with a belly full of turkey club. Maybe it's the fact that we've just removed about three pounds from our backpack, or maybe it's the perfect combination of salty, tangy crunchiness that buoys us down the slope.

---

**Makes 1 sandwich**

2 tablespoons Honey Dijon Aioli

3 slices (yes, three!) sourdough bread, toasted

3 leaves romaine lettuce

2 ounces sliced, roasted deli turkey

3 strips crispy bacon

½ avocado, sliced

½ tomato, sliced

Spread the aioli on one side of all three slices of bread.

Next, because we firmly believe that the correct layering of ingredients is what makes the turkey club so special, assemble the sandwich in the following layers: bread on the bottom; then lettuce, turkey, bacon, avocado; bread; tomato, turkey, lettuce; and bread on the top.

**SKID HACK:** If you, like us, love adding bacon to your sandwiches, we recommend cooking up at least 6 to 8 pieces at a time to stash in the fridge for up to one week, for an easy addition to any sandwich. Everything's better with bacon.

SUMMIT SANDWICHES

# GRILLED HALLOUMI AND HARISSA

Halloumi on a ski tour? Why not? Maybe it sounds a little indulgent, or maybe you're thinking: *What is halloumi?* No shame in not knowing. It's not the most conspicuous cheese in US mountain towns. Kind of like a saltier version of Indian-style paneer, halloumi is a sturdy (often described as squeaky) goat or sheep cheese that originated in the Mediterranean island of Cyprus. Since it has a high melting point, this tasty cheese can easily be pan-fried or grilled—ideal for a skintrack sandwich. It's kind of a splurge at the store, but don't hold back. You're worth it.

**Makes 1 sandwich**

2 tablespoons extra-virgin olive oil, divided

¼ cup finely sliced white or yellow onion

3 ounces halloumi, cut into ½-inch slices

2 slices focaccia

2 tablespoons harissa paste

Handful of arugula

2 tablespoons Spicy Aioli

Heat 1 tablespoon of the olive oil in a cast iron skillet over medium.

Add the onion and sauté until it becomes translucent and starts to caramelize, 6 to 8 minutes.

Remove the onions and set aside. Add the remaining 1 tablespoon olive oil to the pan.

Pan-fry the halloumi slices until browned on both sides, 2 to 3 minutes per side. Remove the slices and set aside.

Toast both sides of the focaccia slices in the pan for 1 to 2 minutes. Alternatively, just toss the focaccia into the toaster while you pan-fry the halloumi, if you want to multitask.

Spread the harissa paste on the bottom slice, then layer the halloumi, caramelized onions, and arugula.

Spread aioli on the top slice and close 'er up.

Slice in half and wrap in foil for the trail.

**SKID HACK:** If you have extra halloumi, cube it, pan-fry it, and dip it into our Miso Peanut Sauce!

# CLASSIC CAPRESE

Italians have created some masterpieces of culinary art, but in the salad department, nothing beats the simple caprese salad. Of course, salads aren't the most portable, so some ingenious Italian skier once decided to load it all onto a slice of focaccia and impress his friends atop some Alpine peak—or so we've heard. Whether that's accurate or not, we know one thing to be true: this classic caprese sandwich won't disappoint, whether it's devoured on that summit or at your kitchen table.

**Makes 1 sandwich**

Splash of extra-virgin olive oil

2 slices focaccia, lightly toasted

2 tablespoons Everyday Pesto

4 ounces fresh mozzarella, sliced

½ tomato, sliced

Handful of basil, roughly chopped

Drizzle the olive oil on the inside of the focaccia.

Spread the pesto on the bottom slice.

Layer the mozzarella and tomato slices on the bottom half.

Garnish with basil.

Close the sandwich and wrap it up if you plan to take it on the trail.

# IN KYRGYZSTAN, SIMPLER IS BETTER
## JOHN PLACK

On a week-long backcountry touring trip to Kyrgyzstan, we weren't quite sure what we'd get for packed lunches. But our guest house's chef, Nurgul, did not disappoint. On a long ski tour to a zone in the Tian Shan mountains called Austrian Kiss, we were overheating in the spring sun. Minutes away from collectively bonking (before we even reached the base of the couloir), it was time to eat. To our delight, the simple sandwiches Nurgul packed in our to-go lunch bags were some of the best skintrack snacks we ever had.

Here's the recipe: Between slices of untoasted whole wheat bread, layer 1 fried egg (yolk cooked firm to prevent a mess), 1 slice of carved turkey or chicken (dark meat, preferably), 1 lettuce leaf, and several cucumber slices. Sprinkle with salt and pepper, wrap it, and stash it in your pack.

*Based out of Vail, Colorado, John Plack is a PR guy for some of your favorite Rocky Mountain ski resorts. He's a former helicopter pilot and amateur endurance athlete who is always looking for far-out places to ski tour.*

# TURKEY, APPLE, BRIE, AND HONEY SANDWICH

One baguette sandwich recipe wasn't enough, so we felt morally obligated to include another take from the French Alps. Strolling the streets of our favorite French town, we couldn't resist these sandwiches beckoning to us through the window of every bakery we passed. While traditionally made with *jambon* (ham), we found a few layered instead with turkey that were even better! We each enjoyed one whole sandwich (too delicious to share) while skiing down from the Argentière Valley after Max proposed. In short, this is a sandwich that will always bring a smile to our faces!

**Makes 1 sandwich**

1 (12-inch) baguette

2 teaspoons unsalted butter

4 ounces roasted turkey breast, sliced

2 ounces brie, sliced

¼ apple, sliced (we like Pink Lady for its tartness, but any will do)

Handful of arugula

Drizzle of honey

Slice open the baguette lengthwise, leaving one long edge intact.

Spread the butter onto the bottom slice.

Layer the bottom slice with the turkey, brie, and apple slices.

Top with arugula and drizzle with honey.

Close the sandwich, package, and stash in your pack.

SUMMIT SANDWICHES 129

# THE TRAM WAFFLE

In Jackson Hole, tram waffles are as iconic as any ski run. On a freezing storm day, when the wind is howling and the snow is hammering sideways, there's nothing better than hiding out in Corbet's Cabin and enjoying a crispy waffle lathered with Nutella or brown-sugar butter. Hey, if you time it right, you might even get an extra one for free! Since there's no Corbet's Cabin everywhere, here's a quick and easy way to enjoy a version of these treats anywhere that's not Rendezvous Mountain.

**Makes 1 waffle sandwich**

2 freezer waffles, toasted

¼ cup Nutella, store-bought or homemade

½ banana, sliced

2 slices bacon, cooked

Lather each waffle thickly with Nutella.

Add the banana slices and bacon to one waffle.

Top with the other waffle to form a sandwich, and package in aluminum foil.

## NORWEGIAN WAFFLES: THE PERFECT SKI FUEL

### SHANE ROBINSON

Norway knows a thing or two about skiing. But what Norway really has figured out is that waffles go with skiing. Waffles as a pre-ski breakfast, of course. And what about a waffle wrapped around an omelet for the best egg sandwich you've ever had? Yes, please. Chocolate-dipped waffle for that extra-sugary, mid-ski snack? Um, I'll take two! Gas-station waffle wrapped around a hot dog? And of course, the best of all, the waffle bar at the Lofoten Ski Lodge, where they have this perfect cream that's just a touch tangy and not too sweet, with a selection of jams and the famous caramelized Norwegian brown cheese. Please, take my money!

*Shane Robinson is the owner of Graybird Guiding and has an insatiable appetite for powder skiing and trail snacks. He has two guiding philosophies in the mountains and in life: (1) lunch is an all-day activity; and (2) always eat your best food, then you are always eating your best food!*

# SKID LUXURY FRENCH TOAST PB&J

Indulgent. That's what we call this spruced-up PB&J. We'd be lying if we said we didn't throw together a classic PB&J every so often, but you don't need us to tell you how to whip one of those up (and yes, spreading peanut butter and jam on a sandwich is totally cooking if you want it to be). Since we're all about going beyond skid, we figured, why not uplevel a classic and enjoy a few of our favorite things in one sandwich? This isn't exactly your running-out-the-door-need-lunch-ASAP sandwich, but if you make the french toast the night before, you can slap this sandwich together in no time.

**Makes 1 sandwich**

½ cup coconut milk, or your preferred milk

1 egg

2 teaspoons maple syrup

½ teaspoon ground cinnamon

Dash of vanilla extract

1 tablespoon coconut oil

2 slices challah bread

2 tablespoons peanut butter (we like crunchy, but you're an adult—do what you please)

2 tablespoons jam, such as Quick Plum Rhubarb Jam

½ banana, sliced

In a deep plate or baking pan, whisk together the milk, egg, maple syrup, cinnamon, and vanilla.

Heat the coconut oil in a large cast iron skillet over medium-high heat.

Dip each slice of bread into the milk mixture, making sure both sides are coated.

Place each slice in the pan and cook until browned, about 2 minutes per side.

Remove the french toast and let cool on a plate or cooling rack.

Once cool, spread the peanut butter on one slice of bread and arrange the banana slices on top.

Lather the jam on the other piece of bread, close the sandwich, and slice in half.

Pack it up and enjoy this upleveled PB&J on a frozen mountaintop.

# KIMCHI GRILLED CHEESE

This recipe has a bit of a funny story behind it. On a long, late-night plane ride to a ski trip in Alaska, a dear friend of ours struck up a conversation about what would be considered acceptable food to bring on an airplane. The debate raged on for hours, taking into consideration the smell, messiness, size, and how much garbage the meal would create. Would you open a can of tuna aboard a flight? What about a jar of kimchi? Thoughts and opinions were exchanged, but the group ultimately did *not* come to a consensus. Yep, we get it, kimchi can be pretty pungent, but get the right brand, and it pleasantly adds some delicious depth to a very simple sandwich—the classic grilled cheese. It's easy to prepare a few of these for your crew on a big day in the mountains or (Max stands by this) a long flight to a faraway adventure.

**Makes 1 sandwich**

2 slices of sourdough bread

2 teaspoons unsalted butter

2 ounces sharp cheddar, sliced

1 ounce jack cheese, shredded

¼ cup of your favorite kimchi (we're big fans of the Trader Joe's kimchi)

1 tablespoon of your favorite hot sauce

Preheat a small skillet over medium heat.

Spread the butter on one side of each slice of bread, then press butter-side down onto the hot skillet to brown and toast, 1 minute.

Keeping your bread in the skillet, carefully sprinkle the shredded jack cheese over one slice of bread and lay the cheddar slices across the other slice.

When the cheese starts to melt, after 3 to 4 minutes, add the kimchi and a dash of hot sauce atop the melted cheeses.

Once the bread is nicely browned, carefully stack one side of the sandwich on top of the other and press together with a spatula.

Flip the sandwich, turn off the heat, and let grill for 2 minutes more.

Remove the sandwich from the skillet, cut in half, and serve (or let cool and package tightly in foil for later).

SUMMIT SANDWICHES 135

# THE BACKCOUNTRY BABES' BAGUETTE

### SHELBY SMITH

This one goes out to all of my backcountry ladies. Say goodbye to the dread you face ten hours into a long ski mission, when you have to choose between a smooshed, dry PB&J and a crumbling energy bar. The pressures of our world can make eating as a woman hard enough—please don't make me eat another stale nut bar. This two-foot-long sandwich empowered me to be a strong mountain lady and use my body to climb to the places that make me the happiest, and I hope it does the same for you. Do yourself a favor and pair this meal with a Snickers bar.

**Step 1:** Acquire a fresh baguette. The better the baguette, the better day you're going to have. If you find yourself in Bozeman, Montana, I highly suggest meandering to Wild Crumb. (Get a huckleberry scone while you're there!)

**Step 2:** Cut said baguette in half, hotdog style. Make sure one of the long ends is still attached, or you're going to have one sloppy sandy.

**Step 3:** Slather mayo on both sides of the baguette. I repeat, no longer do we have to eat dry sandwiches.

**Step 4:** Take a big ole slab of tofu and press with a clean-ish towel until it's dry. Yes, plain tofu. Stick with me here. Cut into slabs. Shovel tofu into baguette.

**Step 5:** Grab your favorite jar of kimchi. Put a bunch of this on top of the tofu slices.

**Step 6:** Top with barbecue sauce, like Bachan's Japanese barbecue sauce, or experiment with using teriyaki sauce, soy sauce, or Miso Peanut Sauce. Let your inner top chef shine here.

**Step 7:** Sprinkle salt flakes on top. You'll thank me later.

**Step 8:** Climb a mountain of your choice, thank the mountain goddesses, and find a beautiful view to eat your full-baguette sandwich. Caution, you might do a happy dance after.

*After living in the Sierras, Rockies, and Alaska and Brooks Ranges, Shelby settled into the Bridgers in Bozeman, Montana, with her boyfriend, Ben, and puppy, Bergschrund. When she's not working to solve climate change, you'll catch her sniffing wildflowers, making kick turns, or bushwhacking with a baguette sandwich sticking out of her pack.*

*Backcountry skier Laura Gaylord ripping a deep powder turn in the Tetons. (Photo by Nick Braun)*

SUMMIT SANDWICHES 137

# POCKET DILLAS, FOUR WAYS

What's even better than a slice of pocket pizza? Pocket quesadillas! Impossible to smoosh—because they're already flat. Turns out that the simplest of Mexican street foods is the ultimate pick-me-up on the skintrack. Walking the streets of Oaxaca or Mexico City, where every corner seemingly has a quesadilla cart serving up sizzling hot, cheesy treats, we quickly learned that quesadillas are just as good if you shove them into a pack and eat them a few hours later. The key to a good quesadilla is the cheese itself, but we've even got a sweeter option that skips dairy altogether. We prefer the portability of corn tortillas, but go big and sub in a large flour tortilla and double up on the filling, if you like.

**Makes 2 quesadillas**

## BEAN AND CHEESE

4 corn tortillas

2 ounces cheddar or jack cheese, sliced

¼ cup refried beans

½ sweet potato, cubed and roasted

## THE ITALIAN

4 corn tortillas

2 tablespoons Everyday Pesto

2 tablespoons goat cheese

2 ounces mozzarella, sliced

2 slices tomato

Handful of arugula

## SWEET CHICKEN

4 corn tortillas

½ cup shredded cooked chicken

¼ red bell pepper, thinly sliced

2 ounces cheddar or jack cheese, sliced

## SKID CREPE

4 corn tortillas

1 banana, sliced

2 tablespoons Homemade Nutella

Preheat a large skillet over medium-high heat and add 2 tortillas.

Layer your chosen fillings onto each tortilla.

Once the ingredients begin to melt and soften, top with another tortilla.

Cook for 3 to 4 minutes (1 minute for Skid Crepes), then carefully flip and cook for another 3 minutes (1 minute for Skid Crepes).

Remove from the heat, let cool, and package for transport.

SUMMIT SANDWICHES 139

# THE BROOKLYN ITALIAN

Some call it a hero, others call it a sub or a hoagie or a grinder. We're going to keep it simple and stick with "delicious Italian sandwich." Growing up in New York City, Max got his fair share of opportunities to visit bustling Italian delis all over the five boroughs and fuel long bike rides and urban exploration missions with delicious sandwiches. The heavily accented NYC Italian guys behind the counter put so much love into their product—the perfect combo of savory flavor and kick of crunchy freshness—it's impossible to fuhgeddaboudit. These days, Max gladly carries one of these loaded sandwiches up a mountain, anticipating that first bite on the summit.

**Makes 1 sandwich**

3 tablespoons Sundried Tomato and Olive Tapenade

1 italian sub roll, sliced lengthwise and lightly toasted

2 ounces sliced genoa salami

2 ounces sliced prosciutto

4 ounces (½ ball) fresh mozzarella, sliced

Handful of arugula

1 tablespoon extra-virgin olive oil

1 teaspoon balsamic vinegar

Spread the olive tapenade on the bottom half of the sub roll.

Layer on the salami, prosciutto, and mozzarella. Top with the arugula.

Lightly drizzle the olive oil and balsamic vinegar over the fillings.

Close the sandwich with the top half of the roll, wrap it for the trail, and make exaggerated Italian hand gestures to indicate it's ready.

# BAKED GOODS

Baked treats are the quickest way to both of our hearts. Anytime we visit a new place, with skis or without, a local bakery is one of our first stops. On trips to ski in the Alps, we've been known to load up our ski packs with half a dozen baked goods—a *pain au chocolat* and almond croissant cushioned carefully between puffy jackets, baguettes strapped to the outside.

Whether it's a hunk of your favorite banana bread (see Bribery Banana Bread) or a zesty citrus loaf (see Lemon Yogurt Cake), homemade baked goods add a welcome slice of comfort to a day in the mountains. We're big proponents of bringing enough to share—that's how lifelong friendships are made in the mountains.

Marzipan cake, which we've turned into mini-muffin-sized cakes for this book, is a consistent favorite among our friends in the Tetons, the most highly requested birthday cake (anyone who knows Lily is allowed to request a baked good of choice on their birthday), and one that consistently gets polished off no matter how large the dinner party. One night, in the middle of ski season, we hosted a handful of friends for dinner, serving up marzipan cake for dessert, only to watch our calm, (mostly) respectful acquaintances turn into sugar-starved pirates as they fought over the last crumbs stuck to the pan. It was only right to turn that cake into a ski snack. Every time we enjoy these bite-sized, marzipan treats in the snow, we think of our goofy friends who inspire us to always pursue new ways to consume elaborate forms of sugar—especially during ski season.

*Opposite: Celebrating Lily's favorite food group (cookies) in the Tetons*

# LEMON YOGURT CAKE

Having a quick one-bowl cake in your back pocket is a secret weapon that will serve you well in life. This zesty yogurt cake fits the bill, with just a few minutes of prep and a sweet reward that will serve as an excellent dinner-party dessert or skintrack snack. In this easy loaf cake, we opt for spelt flour in addition to all-purpose flour and coconut sugar, which add a richer flavor, but feel free to use regular granulated sugar and all-purpose flour, if that's all you have on hand.

You can bake this cake in an eight-inch, round cake pan, if you prefer (decrease cooking time by 10 to 15 minutes), but we like the loaf shape for cakes since it makes them so easy to transport. Plus, there's something about cake in a loaf pan that feels appropriate for eating at all hours of the day. Here's to adding more cake to our lives, whether it's for breakfast, lunch, dinner, or dessert.

---

**Makes one
9-by-5-inch loaf**

1 cup + 2 teaspoons coconut sugar, divided

½ cup plain, full-fat greek yogurt

½ cup extra-virgin olive oil

3 eggs

2 tablespoons lemon zest

1 teaspoon vanilla extract

1 cup all-purpose flour

½ cup spelt flour
(or substitute with
all-purpose flour)

Preheat the oven to 350 degrees F and grease your loaf pan with butter or oil and line with parchment paper.

In a medium bowl, mix 1 cup of the coconut sugar with the yogurt and olive oil until well blended.

Whisk in the eggs and add the lemon zest and vanilla.

Add the flours, baking powder, salt, and turmeric (if using) and stir until just combined (don't overmix!).

1 ½ **teaspoons baking powder**

½ **teaspoon kosher salt**

½ **teaspoon ground turmeric** (optional, for color!)

Pour the batter into the loaf pan and sprinkle the remaining coconut sugar on top.

Bake for 45 to 50 minutes, or until a knife in the center comes out clean. If it's taking longer to cook through, you may have to add foil to the top to prevent the top from browning too much.

# FUDGY ESPRESSO BROWNIES

You already know how we feel about coffee and chocolate. These fudgy brownies are one of our most popular recipes to date, and although they made their debut in our first book, we couldn't resist adding them here, since they've saved our sorry asses on some long pushes in the mountains. In fact, we once traversed twenty-two miles through the Tetons with a big bag of these in our packs. When we were slogging across Jenny Lake as the sun was starting to set, they brought us back to life with a highly necessary caffeine hit that gave us the boost we needed to get back to the car. While we love a warm, gooey brownie, these chocolate hunks taste better after a few days, which makes them ideal for wrapping up and stuffing into a pack for a big adventure.

**Makes 16 brownies**

2 cups white sugar

¾ cup cocoa powder

1 cup unsalted butter, melted

4 eggs

1 teaspoon vanilla extract

1 tablespoon instant coffee

1 ¼ cups all-purpose flour, or ¾ cup oat flour + ½ cup almond flour to make these gluten-free

1 teaspoon kosher salt

**Extra flake salt, to top**

Preheat the oven to 350 degrees F and butter or oil an 8-by-8-inch baking pan.

In a medium bowl, mix the cocoa and sugar.

Add the melted butter to the cocoa-sugar mixture. Mix well.

Stir in the eggs, vanilla, and espresso.

Add the flour and salt and stir until just combined.

Pour the mixture into the baking pan and bake for 45 minutes for extra-gooey results. Sprinkle with flake salt while warm.

Let the brownies cool, wrap them up, and enjoy on a wintery summit!

**SKID HACK:** Don't be afraid to double or triple the coffee suggestion, if you want a little caffeine buzz from these (the small dose is solely for flavor).

# BROWNIES AS CURRENCY

In 2017, five friends and I (Max) planned a ski expedition deep into the mountains of Kluane National Park and Reserve in the northwest corner of Canada. At twenty-two years old, none of us were seasoned mountaineers, but our enthusiasm and a lot of free time had us gunning for big objectives on what would be the biggest adventure of our lives thus far.

We packed food for twenty-five days on the glacier, planning to alternate between seven different meals to keep things interesting. We each took our own favorite personal snacks, plus nearly twenty pounds of Clif Bars and energy gels apiece (the result of a friend's sponsorship). On top of all that, we also packed an additional thirty pounds of homemade brownies from Tom's mom—each one individually wrapped in parchment paper and labeled with our names to ensure we split them evenly. I don't remember the exact calorie count for the load, but it was in the hundreds of thousands. A scary sight.

Flying in a bush plane is a weight-conscious affair, and on departure day, we quickly realized that our bags were significantly overweight. We frantically grabbed whatever we deemed nonessential and threw it all in a pile that would remain at the airstrip.

Out on the glacier, we ate well, enjoying our meals and burning through calories like crazy. Springtime ski mountaineering in the Yukon turned out to be harder than it looked to our young and hungry eyes. Energy bars, shot blocks, energy gels, and other science food became daily snacks, desserts, and skintrack fuel, but the real stars of the show were the brownies.

About ten days into the trip, during a massive snowstorm that buried our tents multiple times, we made the tragic discovery that an entire bag of brownies was missing. Accusations started flying as to who had snuck them into their bags or eaten them all. After our tempers settled, we agreed to ration the remaining brownies. We knew they would get us through our toughest battles, not only as a calorie source, but as a simple reminder of home.

By day twenty, as our food supplies were actually starting to run low, the brownies took on almost a mystical form, serving as the highest-value currency to trade for literally anything—rations of whiskey, cooking dinner, reinforcing our snow-cave cooking area, or hanging and organizing gear to dry. Day by day, their value increased, so that by the time we were packing up, a single brownie could have bought an entire deconstruction and subsequent packing up of a tent. I remember agreeing to split the final one while sitting on our bags as the plane touched down on the glacier.

Back at the airstrip, we were ecstatic to find the last bag of brownies hiding underneath the pile. Basking in the glory of a successful three weeks in the backcountry, we ate ourselves sick on the simple joy of homemade baked goods.

The lesson? The homemade treats are always worth the weight.

*Sean Fearon builds a snow wall to protect our camp (and the brownies) from an incoming storm during our trip to Kluane National Park.*

# TRAIL MIX CHOCOLATE CHIP COOKIES

This chocolate chip cookie is our trail-friendly take on a favorite, packed with oats, nuts, and of course, a little bit of candy. Whether you're halfway up a skintrack, lapping your favorite chairlift, or just craving a sweet late-night dessert, these are sure to hit the spot. We like to make them in batches and freeze or refrigerate some of the dough, so we can bake them fresh anytime. The dough will keep in the fridge for up to a week and in the freezer for up to two months (maybe more, but we've always polished it off pretty quick); see Skid Hack. In a pinch, you can also replace the oats, nuts, and candy with 1.5 cups of your favorite store-bought trail mix.

---

**Makes 26 to 30, two-and-a-half-inch cookies**

1 cup (2 sticks) unsalted butter, at room temperature

1 cup brown sugar

½ cup white sugar

2 eggs

1 tablespoon vanilla extract

2 cups all-purpose flour

½ cup whole wheat flour

1 teaspoon baking soda

1 teaspoon kosher salt

½ cup rolled oats

½ cup Reese's Pieces or M&M's

¼ cup roasted peanuts or nut of your choice

Preheat the oven to 350 degrees F.

Beat the butter and sugars in a stand mixer on medium-high or in a large bowl with a hand mixer until creamy, about 2 minutes. (Alternatively, if you don't have an electric mixer, you can do this by hand. It'll take some effort! Or melt the butter to mix with the sugars; in that case, be sure to chill the dough in the fridge for at least an hour prior to baking.)

Beat in the eggs and vanilla until well mixed, about 1 minute more.

Add the flours, baking soda, and salt and mix at medium speed until everything is just combined and no specks of flour are left.

Remove the bowl from the mixing stand and use a wooden spoon to stir in the oats, candy, nuts, chocolate chips, and raisins until evenly distributed.

¼ cup chocolate chips

¼ cup raisins or any other chopped dried fruit

Flake salt, for garnishing

Roll the cookie dough into balls, 2 to 3 tablespoons each, and place at least 2 inches apart on a baking sheet.

Sprinkle with flake salt.

Bake for 11 to 13 minutes, or until golden brown. Let cool completely before packaging for the trail.

**SKID HACK:** Divvy up the cookie dough into balls, freeze on a baking sheet, then stash them in a gallon-sized plastic bag in the freezer. By using this hack, you won't need to wait for a huge hunk of dough to thaw. It makes it easy to bake up just a few cookies in a jiff if you're craving a late-night snack, since they're already portioned out. Plus, if you're in the mood for snacking on cookie dough, you can just pluck one or two balls out from the freezer.

# CINNAMON ROLL FLATBREAD

Long live flat snacks! Our friend Nora Fierman developed these flatbreads in an effort to avoid "snack destruction by crampon." You can stash them in a pack all day and rest easy, knowing they'll look the same at 4:00 p.m. as they did when you stuffed them in there in the morning. Nora says, "These are intentionally pre-squashed, since we all know skids aren't the most delicate creatures out there. And don't be intimidated by the yeast in this recipe! It's skid friendly." Nora is a Vail-based endurance athlete who is passionate about kitchen messes that uncover the latest and greatest in snacking technology. Her company, Neve, offers portable, plant-based nutrition in a resealable pouch that fits in your pocket or bike bibs.

Feel free to add whatever you want to the cinnamon sugar mixture, like nuts, raisins, coconut, or additional spices. If you do add nuts or raisins, the dough will tear when rolling, but it still tastes excellent. For an indulgent ski snack, pair this with Homemade Nutella.

---

**Makes 8 flatbreads**

½ cup lukewarm water

1 teaspoon cane sugar

½ teaspoon active dry yeast

2 cups all-purpose flour, plus more as needed

½ teaspoon baking powder

½ teaspoon kosher salt

½ cup oat milk or other type of milk, plus more as needed

2 tablespoons brown sugar

2 teaspoons ground cinnamon

1 tablespoon unsalted butter or coconut oil, melted

In a small bowl, whisk together the water, sugar, and yeast. Let it sit (proof) for 5 minutes. It will smell nice and start to bubble. If it doesn't, the yeast is dead and you need new yeast. Stir the mixture to ensure the yeast dissolves.

In a large bowl, mix together the flour, baking powder, and salt. Stir in the milk and yeast mixture until well blended.

Once a dough forms, remove it from the bowl onto a lightly floured surface. Knead the dough until smooth and slightly tacky, about 5 minutes. If the dough is too dry, add milk a tablespoon at a time. If it's too wet, add flour a tablespoon at a time.

Return the dough to the bowl, cover the bowl with a clean kitchen towel, and set it in a warm place, like on top of your refrigerator or in the oven with the light on, for 1 hour. It should double in size.

While the dough is rising, mix the brown sugar and cinnamon together and set aside.

Lightly flour a work surface and roll the dough into a rectangle about 24 inches long and 12 inches wide. (If you don't have a rolling pin, use a wine bottle. We know you definitely have one of those.) Lightly flour the rolling pin as needed, to keep the dough from sticking.

Spread the melted butter over the dough, then sprinkle the cinnamon and sugar mixture on top. Starting at the long side, tightly roll up the dough into a long log. Cut the dough into 8 pieces (or customize the size to fit in your pack or pocket, as Nora does).

Flatten each piece with your hands and fold four corners toward the middle. Roll the chunk into a 4-to-5-inch disk and set it on a baking sheet. Repeat with all the chunks. You may need to do this in batches or use two sheets. Then cover the dough with a kitchen towel and let rise for 30 minutes.

Meanwhile, preheat the oven to 400 degrees F. After the second rise, put the flatbread in the oven for about 12 minutes, flipping halfway through. They should be nice and golden. Let cool and wrap for the trail.

# BRIBERY BANANA BREAD

We originally designed this super easy, one-bowl banana bread for bribing the good folks in ski shops to wax our skis and repair our bases. But it also works for bribing your ski partners to meet you at the trailhead extra early or ski another lap when it's just too good to quit. Sometimes a sweet banana-filled nudge is all you need to squeeze a little more fun out of a day in the mountains. A ski-bum-approved one-bowl recipe means you could almost make this one with your eyes closed. Usually, we make two loaves—one for bribing, and one for ourselves. Extra slices freeze well for prepping snacks ahead of time, too.

**Makes one 8-by-4-inch loaf**

2 to 3 ripe medium bananas (about 2 cups mashed)

½ cup (1 stick) unsalted butter, melted

½ cup brown sugar

¼ cup + 2 teaspoons white sugar, divided

1 egg

1 teaspoon vanilla extract

1 teaspoon baking soda

½ teaspoon kosher salt

1 cup all-purpose flour

½ cup whole wheat flour (or substitute with all-purpose flour)

½ teaspoon cinnamon

½ cup chocolate chips

Preheat the oven to 350 degrees F and butter or grease an 8-by-4-inch loaf pan.

In a medium bowl, mash the bananas and stir in the melted butter.

Add the brown sugar, ¼ cup of the white sugar, egg, vanilla, baking soda, and salt. Stir well.

Add the flours and cinnamon, and stir until fully mixed. Gently fold in the chocolate chips.

Pour the mixture into the loaf pan and sprinkle with the remaining 2 teaspoons white sugar.

Bake for 50 to 55 minutes, or until a toothpick comes out clean. Let cool for at least 15 minutes before removing from the pan.

**SKID HACK:** If your baked treat looks like mush, sprinkle powdered sugar over it and turn it into a fancy masterpiece!

BAKED GOODS

# HANDHELD APFELSTRUDEL

Our favorite part about skiing in the Alps is the constant pit stops for pastries and espresso. In fact, we'd say that enjoying a warm apple strudel on the deck of a mountain hut flanked by snowy, jagged peaks is pretty much the pinnacle of ski snacking. Since we can't rely on mountain huts to fuel us mid ski tour, we opted to craft our own portable strudel, a sweet and flaky treat that we recommend digging into early on your tour (otherwise be prepared for pastry flakes to live in your pack for eternity). Premade puff pastry makes this a surprisingly easy treat to cook up. All that's missing is a shot of espresso to wash it down.

---

**Makes 18 hand pies**

2 sheets frozen puff pastry

2 large apples, peeled and finely chopped (we like Granny Smith for their tartness, but any apple will do)

3 teaspoons fresh lemon juice

3 to 4 tablespoons granulated sugar, plus more for topping (depending on your sweetness preference)

1 tablespoon cornstarch

1 teaspoon ground cinnamon

¼ teaspoon ground cloves

Pinch of sea salt

¼ cup finely chopped walnuts

¼ cup raisins

1 egg

1 tablespoon water

Take the puff pastry out of the freezer and let thaw on the counter for 10 to 20 minutes, until you can unfold it without breaking it.

Preheat the oven to 400 degrees F.

In a medium bowl, toss the apples with the lemon juice.

Stir in the sugar, cornstarch, cinnamon, cloves, and salt.

Stir in the walnuts and raisins.

Roll out the puff pastry sheet until the dough is just barely translucent.

Cut each sheet into 9 even pieces.

Whisk an egg in a small ramekin with 1 tablespoon water.

BAKED GOODS 157

Lay out the puff pastry sheets on a baking sheet (you might need to use two) and brush the outer half-inch of all four edges of each pastry with egg wash.

Add a few spoonfuls of apple filling to the center of each piece of pastry and fold the sides up and over so they are slightly overlapping. Carefully flip them over so that the seam side is down.

Brush the rest of the pastry with egg wash and sprinkle with sugar.

Score the tops with a knife to let steam escape.

Bake for 14 to 16 minutes, or until the pastry is golden brown. These are best eaten the day you make them, but they can be stored in a sealed container at room temperature for up to three days.

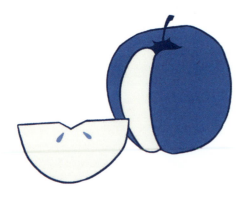

# BRIBE YOUR FRIENDS

## CYNTHIA KRASS

Like a lot of desperate parents, when my kids were little, I frequently bribed them with treats to stay out on the slopes a little longer. Turns out it works with adults, too.

On a week-long backcountry lodge trip in the Esplanade Range of the Selkirks, there was plenty of new snow that looked epic, but all the best pitches were disappointingly and surprisingly windblown. It was fun, but it wasn't magical. I've been chasing powder long enough to recognize magical, and on the third day, we found it in the early afternoon. Most of the crew was tired and even a tad grumpy by the time we dropped into that first truly magical powder run. You know, the kind of snow that makes you feel like you're the best skier who ever lived, and you could go on forever? I finished that run and simply had to do it again. And again and again.

Unfortunately, the crew wasn't totally down with my plan. Over breakfast, we had talked about having a shorter day, and I could tell they were running low on fuel. I whipped out a huge bag of peppermint patties and offered a deal: How about we ski this one more time and you each get a treat? To my surprise, it worked! And in fact, we lapped that area several more times. Each time, my partners said, "Just put another peppermint patty in the slot and I'm good to go!" We skied that zone until we'd tracked up every square inch of fresh snow.

I always carry a supply of treats just in case it's awesome.

*Cynthia (Lily's mom) has developed a reputation for being able to stay out longer than just about anyone when the powder skiing's good. A retired Ironman triathlete with an all-consuming addiction to gravity sports, Cynthia recently entered her seventh decade, and she's only getting faster. You'll hear her before you see her, as most powder turns are accompanied by ear-splitting whoops of joy as she flies down the mountain. Try and have more fun than her, we dare you.*

# MINI ORANGE MARZIPAN CAKES

If there's one thing on a bakery menu that I (Lily) gravitate toward immediately, it's marzipan, a sweet sugar and almond confection. It has a way of turning a simple cake into a decadent one, with a nutty and chewy texture I can live on and never tire of. This cake batter base is a favorite to whip up for a dinner party. Here, it's been adapted to create bite-sized trail cakes to enjoy on snow. We both love the nutty flavor the spelt flour adds, but feel free to substitute any flour, such as all-purpose or whole wheat, in place of the spelt. And thanks to almond flour and marzipan paste, these cakes are easily made gluten-free by swapping gluten-free, all-purpose flour for the spelt.

These dense little cakes are sturdy enough to live in a backpack all day, and they're packed with calories for high-energy needs on the trail. Don't skip the citrus—it's a crucial component to these delicious marzipan treats!

**Makes 16 to 18 mini cakes**

6 tablespoons unsalted butter, room temperature

1 (7-ounce) tube of marzipan paste

½ cup sugar

3 eggs

1 tablespoon orange or lemon zest

1 teaspoon orange or lemon extract

1 cup spelt flour

1 cup almond flour

1 teaspoon baking powder

½ teaspoon kosher salt

Preheat the oven to 350 degrees F and line two 12-cup muffin pans with 18 liners and cooking spray (or make these in two batches).

In the bowl of a stand mixer fitted with the paddle attachment, cream together the butter, marzipan, and sugar on medium speed until light and fluffy.

Beat in the eggs on medium speed until well combined, then add the orange zest and extract and mix on low.

Add the spelt and almond flours, baking powder, and salt, and mix again on low until just combined.

Pour the batter into the muffin liners, filling them about two-thirds full, and bake for 18 to 22 minutes, until a toothpick in the center comes out clean.

Let cool, then store in a sealed container in the fridge for up to one week.

# CHOCOLATE CHAIRLIFT COOKIES

Stuff a bag of these cookies in your jacket pocket and make friends wherever you go. These rich chocolate and olive oil cookies began as a holiday favorite, but have since become a season-long staple. Stir them together in one bowl, chill them in the fridge, and bake for only ten minutes! So easy, even a ski bum can do it, or little kids. If you're totally over the mess of gingerbread houses, whip up a batch of these with kids instead; they're fun to roll out and you can make them as small or large as you want. Plus, they make great bribes on the hill to get your whole family to ski longer.

**Makes 28 to 32 two-inch cookies**

1 cup white sugar

½ cup cocoa powder

¼ cup extra-virgin olive oil

2 large eggs

Mix the sugar and cocoa powder in a medium bowl, then stir in the olive oil.

Whisk in the eggs and vanilla.

Add the flour, baking powder, and salt, and stir until well combined.

2 teaspoons vanilla extract

1 cup all-purpose flour (or ½ cup all-purpose and ½ cup whole wheat)

1 teaspoon baking powder

¾ teaspoon kosher salt

¼ cup powdered sugar

Cover the bowl and refrigerate for at least 3 to 4 hours.

Preheat the oven to 350 degrees F and pour the powdered sugar into a small bowl.

Roll the dough into 1-tablespoon balls and toss them in the powdered sugar until fully coated.

Space the cookies at least 2 inches apart on a baking sheet.

Bake for 10 minutes. The cookies will seem soft and undercooked but will harden up when they cool, so don't be tempted to over bake!

## FOOD AS A LOVE LANGUAGE
### HELEN LEWIS

I have a few ski partners with a larger-than-average aptitude for sharing. These friends always stow away extra treats specifically to share with others during our adventures. At a viewpoint, switchback, summit, or bonk, these small gifts of food are doled out with no ceremony, an accepted part of how these ski partners move through the world. They are my models for practicing gift giving. They remind me that the snacks in my pack are ours—there's no mine or yours. Food is fuel, for sure. Food is also how we build community, and a culture of giving gifts through shared morsels contributes to my own understanding of what it means to give genuinely. Here's to adventures with smoked salmon, date cookies, fresh coffee, miso soup, and chocolate passed to the right.

*Helen Lewis is a Jackson, Wyoming, resident and a former NOLS instructor.*

# SCALLION AND CHEESE WAFFLES

There are many great things about slow waffle mornings. First, it usually means sleeping in (Max's favorite), which is a rarity in our household in the winter. Second, it usually means leftover waffle batter to cook up treats for later adventures. We stir cheese and scallions into our leftover batter for a savory version of Grandma Hilda's Overnight Waffles (a family classic). No offense to maple syrup, but cheese and scallions may be the best waffle addition we can think of. Enjoy these for a second breakfast on a windy summit, or pack a few in your pocket to share in the tram line.

**Makes 8 to 10 waffles**

2 cups whole milk, heated to 105 degrees F

½ cup water, heated to 105 degrees F (see Skid Hack)

2 ¼ teaspoons instant yeast

1 tablespoon white sugar

1 ¼ cups all-purpose flour

¾ cup whole wheat flour

½ cup unsalted butter, room temperature

1 teaspoon kosher salt

2 eggs

¼ teaspoon baking soda

½ cup sharp cheddar cheese, shredded

4 green onions, finely chopped

Sprinkle of ground black pepper

The night before you plan to make waffles, mix the milk, water, yeast, and sugar in a large bowl until the yeast dissolves. (See Skid Hack, below.)

Stir the flours, butter, and salt into the yeast mixture until well blended. Cover and let mixture sit on the counter overnight.

In the morning, beat in the eggs and baking soda until thoroughly mixed.

Stir in the cheese and green onions.

Preheat a waffle iron. Pour batter into the waffle iron and cook according to your waffle iron's instructions.

Eat immediately, or let cool and wrap to throw in your pack.

**SKID HACK:** In order for yeast to activate, the water should be 90 to 105 degrees F. You don't need a thermometer to test this; just put your hand under the faucet. If it feels hot but not so hot that you have to jerk your hand away, it should be in the right range.

Heat the milk a microwave-safe bowl for 30 to 45 seconds, or in a small saucepan until barely hot to the touch. Don't make it too hot or else the yeast will die.

# BACKCOUNTRY BISCUITS

Our friend Katie Matthews, an avid backcountry skier and an aspiring ski guide in Montana, shared this recipe and the backstory with us. The biscuits originated in Nome, Alaska, where Katie's dad was the walrus management biologist. "My dad had these delicious homemade biscuits at a local's home on a cold, dark, snowy evening. He couldn't leave the recipe behind, and neither could I when I left home. A comfort food, a childhood memory, and now a backcountry snack essential that is near and dear to my heart. . . . I hope you will enjoy them as much as I have." Katie's dad is happily retired in the state of Montana. He has been making homemade biscuits since 1977 that are best enjoyed deep in the woods. As a food enthusiast, Katie is always looking for new ways to spice up her backcountry hut meals and share them with friends, family, and yes, even her dog, Sage.

### Makes 20 biscuits

2 cups all-purpose flour

4 tablespoons sugar

3 teaspoons baking powder

Dash of cream of tartar

½ cup shortening or unsalted butter

⅔ cup milk (skim, 2%, or whole)

Preheat the oven to 430 degrees F.

In a large mixing bowl, whisk together the flour, sugar, baking powder, and cream of tartar.

Use your hands or a fork to incorporate chunks of the shortening into the dry ingredients. Mix until the chunks are pea size or smaller.

Add the milk and mix until all the dry ingredients are mixed in and a dough forms.

Sprinkle a bit of flour onto a work surface and knead and fold the dough a few times, until smooth and pliable (don't overknead). Flatten the dough until it's about a ½-inch thick.

Fold the dough in half, doubling its thickness. Cut the dough into 2-inch squares and place on a baking sheet at least 1 inch apart.

Bake for 15 minutes, or until the tops are lightly browned.

Enjoy immediately with butter and honey or jam, or let cool and package for your trip to the mountains. They are best eaten within a few days, but can be frozen for up to one month.

# BUTTER MOCHI CAKE

Lily's aunt Chris has lived on the Big Island of Hawaii since before Lily was born, and visiting her as a kid was always the highlight of Lily's year. We recently went back to visit for the first time in a while (Max's first time to Hawaii!) and discovered the most amazing local treat: butter mochi. It's a mix between a blondie and ball of mochi—sweet, chewy, and incredibly filling.

You can make the whole recipe using just one bowl and a fork to stir. The only hard part is that you'll need mochiko flour—sweet, glutinous rice flour—which is hard to come by if you live in a mountain town. When we're visiting Lily's parents in the Pacific Northwest, we can get it at most Asian grocery stores, but in Jackson, we usually have to order it online. Don't be tempted to sub regular rice flour, which won't create that same sticky consistency.

**Makes 20 to 24 bars**

1 (16-ounce) box of mochiko (sweet rice) flour

2 cups granulated white sugar

1 teaspoon baking powder

½ teaspoon kosher salt

4 large eggs

1 (13.5-ounce) can full-fat coconut milk

½ cup coconut oil, melted

2 teaspoons vanilla extract

Preheat the oven to 350 degrees F and butter or greasea 9-by-13-inch pan.

In a small bowl, whisk together the mochiko flour, sugar, baking powder, and salt.

In a large bowl, whisk together the eggs, coconut milk, coconut oil, and vanilla until well combined.

Stir in the dry ingredients until everything is well combined.

Pour the mixture into the pan.

Bake for 50 minutes, or until a knife in the center comes out clean.

Let cool completely before cutting into bars. Store in a sealed container in the fridge for up to one week.

**SKID HACK:** Imitation vanilla is totally fair game. Our oven is cranking out snacks and treats on the daily, so we're constantly restocking our pantry with baking supplies to have on hand. If we strike it rich one day, we'd love to have a never-ending flow of real-deal vanilla extract on hand, but for now, we often rotate in the pretend stuff. It's a fraction of the price and tastes similar enough. Judge us if you want.

BAKED GOODS 169

# SIPPABLES

It can be hard to stay hydrated in the winter. Nothing sounds worse than sipping cold water on a frosty day in the mountains. Anyone else frequently return home at the end of a winter day with a full water bottle? Plus, water is boring.

As a result, we've spiced up our sippable game with hot soups and teas that warm us from the inside and homemade cold drinks that replenish sodium and add a boost of caffeine when we need it most. Of course, we still like to keep a small amount of plain water on hand, but it's often not our primary source of hydration on the skintrack.

This chapter is a collection of all things liquid—from fun ways to prepare and transport coffee and tea, with our Mudslide Mocha and Dirty Honey Chai Tea; to electrolyte-rich broths (hello, Miso Ramen Broth); a pre-ski smoothie, courtesy of our favorite nutrition therapist; and even some refreshing 21+ options to enjoy from the parking lot while basking in the sun in flip-flops and looking up at the line you just skied.

*Opposite: Sipping miso soup while the sun comes up in the Tetons*

171

# MISO HONEY-LEMON WATER

Perhaps the simplest recipe in the book, this honey-lemon water is a staple for Lily in the winter. She developed this recipe when she was tired of all the tea bags in the pantry one morning. Even when the fridge is especially barren, we can usually scrounge up honey, lemon juice, and miso, which makes for a mild yet replenishing drink that we can sip for hours on end. It's especially comforting on days when it's snowing hard.

**Makes 20 ounces**

20 ounces boiling water

1 tablespoon fresh lemon juice (about ¼ of a lemon)

1 tablespoon honey

1 teaspoon white miso paste, or an extra generous pinch of flake salt

Pour the boiling water into your thermos and add the lemon, honey, and miso. If you want an extra lemony kick, drop a whole lemon slice in your water to infuse while you're on the trail.

Secure the top, shake well, and toss in your backpack.

# SOUL-WARMING CARROT GINGER SOUP

This is the kind of soul-rejuvenating soup that warms you from the inside out, with cozy spices that turn this trail-ready soup into a full-on comfort food. The zing from ginger and umami from a dash of white miso make for one of our all-time favorite soup bases. Cooking dinner one night, we had a realization: Why not take it to go and sip it while trudging through the snow? Give it a good shake before you open up your thermos, since it will definitely separate while it sits in your pack.

**Makes about 3 cups**

1 tablespoon extra-virgin olive oil

½ white onion, finely chopped

1 tablespoon minced ginger

1 clove of garlic, minced

4 large carrots, coarsely chopped

½ teaspoon kosher salt, plus more to taste

1 (13.5-ounce) can full-fat coconut milk

1 cube of veggie bouillon

Ground black pepper

Squeeze of fresh lemon juice

Add the olive oil to a medium saucepan and heat on medium-high.

Add the onion and sauté until fragrant, about 2 minutes.

Add the ginger, garlic, carrots, and salt, reduce the heat to medium, and cook for 5 to 8 minutes, stirring occasionally.

Add the coconut milk and veggie bouillon. Bring the mixture to a boil.

Once boiling, turn the heat to low and let the soup simmer for 20 to 25 minutes, until you can easily puncture the carrots with a fork.

Use an immersion blender to liquefy the soup. It will be pretty thick at this point, so stir in ¼ cup of water at a time to thin it out.

Add black pepper, extra salt to taste, and a squeeze of lemon.

Pour some soup directly into your thermos and store the rest in a sealed container in the fridge for up to one week or in the freezer for one month or more.

 **SKID HACK:** If you have a fancy, high-watt blender, feel free to throw all the ingredients in raw for the quickest, easiest soup.

# MUDSLIDE MOCHA

In addition to powder skiing, chocolate and coffee are right up there on the list of life's greatest pleasures. Since we're often dashing out the door in pursuit of untracked snow, we don't often enjoy slow second-cup mornings. Since drinking less coffee is absolutely not an option, we decided to take cup number two on the road, adding chocolate for a little richness and extra calories. We've been known to finish it before we even get to the ski hill, but if you can hold off and save it for the afternoon, there's no better pick-me-up in the middle of an epic ski day. We're loyal espresso drinkers, but french press or pour-over could work in a pinch.

**Makes one 10-ounce mocha**

1 cup milk (we like oat but any regular or alternative will do)

2 teaspoons cocoa powder

1 teaspoon sugar

1 double shot of espresso, or 2 to 3 ounces of your preferred style of coffee

Add milk, cocoa powder, and sugar to a mug, and microwave it in 30-second increments until warm (alternatively, warm the mixture in a saucepan on the stove over medium-low heat until warm).

Add the espresso and transfer the mocha to a thermos for the road.

**SKID HACK:** Mix a hot cocoa packet with hot water or milk and add a double shot of espresso.

# NEVER UNDERESTIMATE THE POWER OF THE THERMOS

As long as you're moving, it's fairly easy to stay warm in the snow. But the minute you stop, all that sweat freezes, and it can be hard to stay warm on a snack break or summit lunch. The first thing we recommend doing (yes, *before* taking out your snacks) is throwing on a big puffy jacket to trap all that precious heat.

Still, a jacket can only get you so far. Which is why sometimes it's crucial to heat ourselves up from the inside. So the next step is to whip out a thermos. It's easy to look at an insulated thermos as a huge waste of space and weight in an already overstuffed backpack. But a sip of something hot (whether it's sweet or savory) could become the make-or-break point of your day.

One day, while skiing 25 Short in Grand Teton National Park, the skiing was as good as it gets. Our legs were getting heavy, but we couldn't bring ourselves to call it quits. Lap after lap it just kept getting better—fresh snow filling our tracks by the time we got back to the top. On our second-to-last lap, we were drenched and cold. My puffy jacket was soaked with snow, and I (Lily) was running out of tools to keep myself warm as the temps started plummeting. We had plenty of daylight left, but I'd gone from euphoric to miserable in a matter of minutes and was determined to call it quits and head home. Shivering at our high point, I reached for my thermos, which had a few sips of still-hot miso soup left. A few glugs of that hot elixir did the trick. Warmth spread through my body, like getting a hug from the inside, and I was buoyed by a renewed sense of motivation. I downed the rest, and all of a sudden, the world was right. My soggy jacket didn't matter.

We dropped in and skied two more laps.

# DIRTY HONEY CHAI TEA

Warm spices, a boost of espresso . . . what's not to like? We all have mornings when it's a little harder to get moving. Back-to-back ski days, late nights, alpine starts—it can be hard to feel rested during the ski season. But when the storm won't quit, there's no time for sleeping. Fill your thermos with this cozy and energizing tea and chase those powder turns!

**Makes 16 ounces**

1 cup water

1 cup coconut milk

2 chai tea bags

1 tablespoon honey

Generous sprinkle of flake salt

1 double shot of espresso, or 2-to-3 ounces of your preferred style of coffee

Combine the water and coconut milk in a small saucepan.

Add the tea bags and bring the mixture to a boil.

Remove from the heat. Stir in the honey and flake salt.

Remove the tea bags and add the tea to a thermos along with the espresso. Seal and shake well.

SIPPABLES 179

# MISO RAMEN BROTH

Skiing in Japan has its perks: legendary deep powder, a vibrant and fascinating culture, and ramen literally everywhere, from on-mountain cafeterias to vending machines. We couldn't get enough of that electrolyte-laden, soul-warming, rejuvenating miso broth. Make this one at home and take it in a thermos on your midwinter adventure, to enjoy that little boost of energy when things are feeling extra frigid. Store the full batch in your fridge for up to a week and pack a few ounces at a time in a smaller container. Heat it in the microwave or on a stovetop to rewarm before leaving the house.

**Makes 32 ounces**

5 cups water

3 tablespoons white miso paste

½ carrot, thinly sliced

3 ounces shiitake mushrooms, thinly sliced

1 tablespoon dried nori flakes

Bring the water to a boil in a medium saucepan.

Add the miso and carrots, stir, and cook for 5 to 6 minutes, until the carrots soften.

Turn down the heat and let simmer. Toss in the mushrooms and cook for 10 minutes.

Remove from the heat and pour into your thermos immediately, or refrigerate in a jar for up to one week.

Sprinkle nori flakes into the broth before serving.

**SKID HACK:** You can find miso soup packets at most grocery stores, and they make for a deliciously salty, soul-warming sip on a winter's day.

# ICED EARL GREY MAPLE TEA

There's nothing like a hot thermos of tea on a cold day. But not all days in the mountains are frigid. When spring skiing rolls around, it can be tough to replenish lost electrolytes as you sweat. This cold, salty tea hits all the categories we look for in a homemade electrolyte drink: sugar, salt, and a little bit of caffeine. It's wildly refreshing, a welcome sip both on the skin-track and poured over ice at the trailhead.

**Makes 32 ounces**

4 cups boiling water
3 earl grey tea bags
Juice from ½ a lemon
1 tablespoon maple syrup
Hearty sprinkle of flake salt

In a large glass measuring cup or mug, pour the boiling water over the tea bags and steep for 5 minutes.

Remove the tea bags and add the lemon juice, maple syrup, and salt.

Let the mixture cool, then refrigerate overnight.

Store in the fridge and fill your thermos before heading out the door.

# THE ITALIAN

A true staple of Alps skiing, an afternoon shot of espresso will make you unstoppable. It's best served by an Italian *nonna*, who's been in charge of the same mountain hut for five decades, with a huge smile and whatever piece of cake looks best.

*Optional:* Channel your inner Italian mountain guide and smoke a cigarette while passing everyone on the skintrack.

---

**1 single shot of espresso**

**Dash of white sugar**

Pull a shot of espresso into a small thermos. Stir in sugar, seal, and hit the slopes.

# CHUNKY MONKEY SMOOTHIE

This smoothie is great the morning of a big day in the mountains. A morning when you're so excited and crunched for time that you don't feel hungry at all, but you know your body needs fuel to feel energized during the first few hours.

Our friend and nutrition therapist Kaylee shared this recipe with us. She explains, "A room-temperature, blended smoothie is easy for the body to digest and doesn't shock the system the way a cold smoothie does. The sugars are soothing, helping your body relax, and they deliver quick energy to your brain, muscles, and lungs as you start moving on the trail. The protein and fat take longer to digest and will provide sustained energy for at least an hour into your day." The best part: you can drink your smoothie on the way to the trailhead.

**Makes 1 smoothie**

4 tablespoons chia seeds

1 ½ to 2 cups unsweetened vanilla almond milk, divided

1 banana

¼ cup full-fat, unsweetened greek yogurt

1 tablespoon almond butter

1 to 2 tablespoons cocoa powder

Mix the chia seeds with 1 cup of the almond milk in a small bowl or jar. Let stand for at least 2 hours, or overnight, in the refrigerator.

In a blender, put ½ cup of the almond milk, the banana, yogurt, almond butter, cocoa powder, and chia pudding and blend until smooth. Add more almond milk if needed to achieve your desired consistency.

Pour into a container with a lid and head for the hills.

# THE SPAGHETT OR THE SKID SPRITZ

Our friend Ariel tells us this is literally the easiest "cocktail" you can make. We agree. Bonus points if you ask your local watering hole to add this to the menu (as Ariel did) *and they do* (shout-out to the Mangy Moose in Jackson)! Ariel says, "Let's spread this to ski resorts and bike parks across the land." If you can't get Miller High Life in a glass bottle, which Ariel insists upon, some other domestic beer will do in a pinch.

Ariel "Harry" Kazunas has been an accomplice (often an instigator) for many of our dumb and not-so-dumb ideas over the past five years. We first met her on a camping trip in Montana, where she showed up with a full traveling bar in the back of her Toyota Tacoma, whipping up delicious creations for the whole crew after an all-day bike ride. We immediately knew we'd become fast friends. While Ariel is known to craft a mean cocktail, she also brings kindness and goofiness to every adventure we have in the mountains, embodying what it means to take care of each other. Ariel describes herself as a "professional lurker and freelance writer based in Wydaho, whose passions include skiing, mountain biking, babying her houseplants, advocating for housing justice, and smashing the patriarchy." Fun fact: she also officiated our wedding!

---

**Makes 1 cocktail**

1 ice cold Miller High Life in a *glass bottle*

1 shot Aperol

1 slice and/or bit of peel of a lemon or an orange

Sip just enough of the High Life to make room for the Aperol shot.

Pour the Aperol into the bottle.

Add your citrus of choice.

Bask in the glow of your own glory.

SIPPABLES 189

# THE OLDER BUT NOT GROWN-UP OLD FASHIONED

Heading on a hut trip? Car camping in Moab? Then you obviously already packed whiskey and maple syrup. Only thing left to throw in is a small, easy-to-pack bottle of bitters. With this little bottle, you'll have yourself a fancy beverage that puts everyone else's warm beer to shame. Ariel says, "Using *real* maple syrup is critical here—we're talking stuff from Vermont or Massachusetts or Canada, not the stuff made from Iowa corn! Also, life is short, babes, buy nice booze." This cocktail tastes best in a steamy yurt surrounded by friends and drying boot liners.

**Makes 1 cocktail**

2 ounces whiskey or bourbon

½ ounce real maple syrup, plus more to taste

Dash of bitter and/or orange bitters

Orange peel and/or maraschino cherry

Ice or an icicle

Add the whiskey to a sturdy, pleasing-to-hold vessel. This is an often overlooked part of making any cocktail, but its importance should not be underestimated.

Stir in the maple syrup; add more to taste.

Add a few splashes of bitters and/or orange bitters (Ariel prefers both).

Rub the orange peel along the rim of the glass and drop it into the cocktail, to really get that bougie essence in every sip.

Add a cherry if you're feeling extra. (Ariel is always extra.)

Add ice or an icicle, if handy, and stir.

# THE CORPSE REVIVER

At first glance, it looks like you'll have to purchase a number of spirits you aren't likely to use again to make this cocktail. But then you make one. And suddenly it seems very easy to go through those not-so-weird-anymore bottles quite quickly. Ariel says it's "perfect for spring days on decks when you're back early from a corn harvest and feel like you need to put some pep back in your step. Or for after bike rides in the sun on the Loop Road in Grand Teton National Park, when your friend Molly busts out her pizza oven in the trailhead parking lot and you need a beverage to complement the delicious absurdity of it all."

The lemon juice is critical here! Don't bother with the squeezy-bottle lemon juice that tastes like sour plastic. Shell out and get either real lemons or the high-quality bottled stuff. Seriously. This will make or break the drink. The cocktail is best served in a chilled coupe glass, but if you don't have one, a highball glass will suffice.

---

**Makes 1 cocktail**

Absinthe, for rinse

1 ounce gin

1 ounce Lillet Blanc

1 ounce orange liqueur (such as Cointreau or Grand Marnier)

1 ounce fresh or bottled organic lemon juice

Ice, for chilling

Pour a splash of absinthe in a glass, swirl it around a little, and dump. (Alternatively, if the absinthe rinse feels too wasteful, add a tiny splash of absinthe to the mix.)

Combine the gin, Lillet, orange liqueur, and lemon juice in a shaker with ice and shake to chill the cocktail. If you don't have a shaker (get one!), you can just stir the ice into the cocktail and then pour the drink into a glass, or mix it in a glass and add an ice cube.

Sip, and enjoy being resurrected!

# SALTED MAPLE ICED COFFEE

This is Ariel's favorite way to use up extra coffee on group hut or camping trips. "It's the tastiest way to electrolyte yourself after you've put out a lot of physical effort but still have to go to work or give public comment or something. Maple syrup is nature's perfect food. It's got a ton of potassium, calcium, iron, manganese, and a whole bunch of other good stuff hidden under that delicious nectar-of-the-gods taste. So for the love of those gods, never ever buy anything other than 100% pure maple syrup." You can use any type of milk here. We use oat milk. Ariel prefers a mix of half-and-half and oat milk.

*Optional:* Freeze this in popsicle form for hot days!

---

**Makes about 10 to 12 ounces**

8 ounces coffee

2 tablespoons pure maple syrup

¼ teaspoon kosher salt

2 to 3 ounces milk or milk substitute

Ice, for serving

Mix the coffee with the maple syrup and salt. Add more syrup and salt to taste.

Stir in the milk till it's as creamy as you like it.

Ice, ice it baby and enjoy.

# SALTED MAPLE LEMONADE

Caffeine not your thing? This post-adventure beverage, developed by our friend Ariel, takes advantage of all of maple syrup's many benefits but substitutes hydrating water and vitamin-C-heavy lemon juice for coffee. The quantities listed here are a general starting point. Modify to taste, and size up if you need to make more than one serving. Fresh lemon juice is best here, but if you opt for the bottled stuff, use a high-quality brand, like Santa Cruz Organic.

**Makes 1 cup**

1 cup water

2 tablespoons pure maple syrup

1 tablespoon fresh lemon juice

¼ teaspoon kosher salt

Ice (optional)

Stir together the water, maple syrup, lemon juice, and salt.

Add ice, if desired, and feel the life flow back into your soul with every sip.

# TAILGATE TREATS

Have you ever gotten back to the car after a daylong winter adventure and *not* been hungry? Turns out that après-ski is as essential as the skiing itself. Huge shock? Not really.

The thing is, when you get back from a long day out, there's probably nothing you want to do less than cook. That's why, over the years, we've perfected the art of simple après snacks that you can enjoy right on the tailgate of your truck. On a sunny spring day, there's nothing better than peeling off your ski boots and kicking back in a camp chair with a cold beverage, hearty snacks, and a pair of comfy shoes to bask in the glow of the jagged range.

All of these snacks can be prepped the evening before for easy transport and enjoyment after your big day. Wrecked from a hard effort and need some refreshment? The Chocolate-Blueberry Recovery Smoothie will breathe life back into your tired legs. Better yet, want to impress the friends you just shared a massive spring corn couloir with? Fire up your portable pizza oven and bake a few crowd-pleasing Tailgate Pizzas. Just remember to carry out what you carry in, and leave no trace!

*Opposite: Loading gear into a mountain taxi in Santa Caterina, Italy before a five-day hut-to-hut ski trip in the Alps*

# CHOCOLATE-BLUEBERRY RECOVERY SMOOTHIE

There are many schools of thought on how we should fuel ourselves while we ski. Some eat a little, some eat a lot; but one thing that's pretty universally agreed upon is how important a recovery meal is, ideally within the first thirty minutes of finishing your effort. This delicious smoothie is an easy way to check that box. Blitz it up at home the night before or morning of your outing, and stash it in the car for a tasty post-ski recovery drink that will at least tide you over until your next meal. Give the smoothie a good shake before you sip. It tends to separate while sitting in the car.

## TIPS FOR WINTER PICNICS AND TAILGATING

The most important element to consider when setting up a winter picnic or tailgate is the weather. Gusty winds or frosty temps can quickly turn an idyllic hangout into a total sufferfest. We definitely prefer picnicking in the snow after March rolls around. . . . But if you're motivated midwinter, pack some extra layers and bring hot beverages.

If you're planning a mountainside picnic, pack an extra puffy jacket (or two), so you can comfortably chill out for a while. Having something to sit on instead of the snow, whether it's your backpack or a purpose-brought square of closed-cell foam, will also make a huge difference.

For tailgating post-ski, an extra pair of dry socks is crucial, as are extra layers and maybe a large blanket. We have a wool blanket that lives in the back seat of our truck, a wedding gift that we use as a picnic blanket or bust out almost every time we tailgate with friends.

For a tailgate, foldable camping chairs with some back support are everything. We keep two or three stashed in the bed of our truck for post-ski hangs, because if everyone's comfortable, we're more likely to extend our hangout.

**Makes one 12-ounce smoothie**

1 serving of chocolate protein powder (either one or two scoops, depending on the brand)

1 banana

½ cup soy milk or your milk of choice, plus more as needed

½ cup water

½ cup chopped strawberries

¼ cup blueberries

1 tablespoon creamy peanut butter

Handful of spinach

Add all ingredients to your blender.

Blend until smooth. Add a bit more milk if needed to achieve your desired consistency.

Store in a thermos or mason jar and stash in the car for a post-ski refuel.

# BERRY CHIA YOGURT PARFAIT

We could all use more breakfast in our lives. Maybe it's because we often spend traditional breakfast time climbing uphill with our headlamps on or nomming toast behind the steering wheel. Whatever the reason, we suggest never turning down a chance for breakfast. Even if it's at 4:00 p.m. This parfait really hits the spot after a sunny spring tour. It's a refreshing snack that holds up well for hours in the car. Both of us always miss fresh fruit when out on a long day, so why not stage some for immediate consumption upon return? If you plan to enjoy a parfait on a warm spring day, we recommend stashing it in a cooler in the car.

**Makes 1 parfait**

½ cup plain greek yogurt

1 tablespoon honey

1 tablespoon Quick Plum Rhubarb Jam

⅓ cup fresh berries of your choice

1 tablespoon chia seeds

¼ cup granola

Put the greek yogurt in a portable container.

Layer the honey and jam on top but do not mix.

Next add berries, then chia seeds, then granola. Put the lid on and stash in the car or cooler.

# THE MATT DILLON SPECIAL

The late March sun hung low in the sky, dipping below the snowcapped Selkirk peaks. It was well past a reasonable time to get back from a backcountry ski tour, but hut skiing rules are different. Especially at the Sentry Lodge.

Jelly-legged and filled to the brim with joy from an eleven-hour day of powder skiing, I (Lily) kicked off my ski boots and slid into the long wooden bench seat next to my exhausted ski partners. We'd missed appetizer hour, but Chef Matt Dillon had kindly saved us "something small."

That "small" treat was a *tarte flambée*, a buttery, flaky pastry topped with gruyère, radicchio, ham, and a drizzle of honey.

"I think this is the best thing I've ever had in my entire life," I sighed, ogling the perfectly browned crust sparkling with honeyed, melted cheese.

"Oh, like the best tarte you've ever had?" asked Matt.

"No, like the best thing. Period," I clarified, reaching for another piece.

It was day five of an unimaginably indulgent seven days at the Sentry Lodge near Golden, British Columbia, a heli-access backcountry ski lodge.

Matt, a friend of trip organizer Shane Robinson, had spent the past few days serving up the kind of meals one can only dream about. Roasted lamb from his farm on Washington's Vashon Island, foraged nettles and wild mushrooms, sushi-grade tuna, homemade miso soup, latkes for breakfast with smoked salmon eggs, homemade sourdough bread, fresh croissants. Matt handed us bento box lunches as we left the lodge each day, surprising us with meals like kimchi fried rice and decadent sandwiches to savor while snow flurried around us.

"Matt likes to cook in themes," Shane hinted to us while we opened up our skintrack lunches one day to find udon with shrimp, veggie slaw, and a homemade egg roll.

First breakfast, second breakfast, lunch, appetizers, and dinner left absolutely nothing to be desired. In fact, it was a blessing that we spent eight to eleven hours ski touring each day, because each pang of hunger brought with it the feeling of opportunity—the opportunity to indulge in the next Matt Dillon creation.

200  SKI SNACKS

Indulging on the skintrack fuels the body and soul. But it's often the food we enjoy right after we've peeled off our boots—euphoric after an amazing day and ravenous for something salty—that tastes the best. And if, by chance, you spent the day survival skiing through breakable crust or rattling your fillings out on frozen crud, that après treat might even put a 180-degree spin on an otherwise crappy day on skis.

I can't claim that any of our Tailgate Treats compare to the magic of a Matt Dillon Special, but I do hope the same sentiment carries through: the importance of taking a moment to sit down, bask in the glory of the day, and enjoy something delicious to cap off a day on snow.

*One of the many delicious skintrack lunches Matt Dillon packed with love at the Sentry Lodge. It doesn't get better than homemade egg rolls, shrimp, and udon noodles, complete with chopsticks.*

# CHARCUTERIE BOARD

It's no secret that Europeans love their cured meats and cheeses, and that's certainly one of our favorite parts of skiing in the Old World. Unfortunately, we don't have the same infrastructure of *rifugios* here in the States, but the next best thing is getting back to the parking lot and digging into a spread of treats you've artfully laid out for your crew. It doesn't really matter what it's served on (get creative and use whatever you have around, or remember to pack your favorite cutting board).

What's crucial is the selection of ingredients. We like to balance the various meats and cheeses with crackers, bread, jam, and some pickles to really round it out. Get creative with what's available, but here's a great place to start!

---

**Makes 1 board that serves 4 to 6**

1 (8-ounce) spicy salami stick, thinly sliced, or 8 ounces presliced salami

8 ounces thinly sliced prosciutto

4 ounces sharp white cheddar

4 ounces manchego cheese

1 (8-ounce) log of goat cheese

1 (8-ounce) brie wheel

12 to 15 cornichon pickles

1 baguette, thickly sliced

¼ cup Sundried Tomato and Olive Tapenade

¼ cup Quick Plum Rhubarb Jam

Clean your serving platform, you skid!

Lay out your meats, cheeses, and accoutrements.

Serve the tapenade and jam in small bowls for dipping.

TAILGATE TREATS 203

# TAILGATE PIZZA, THREE WAYS

Pizza parties aren't just for corporate retreats or preteen birthdays. We believe they're best at the trailhead or base-area parking lot after a big day of spring skiing. These recipes rely on a portable, propane-fired pizza oven, so either get one of your own, or find a buddy to mooch off. Get that flame roaring and bake up some pies on the tailgate to enjoy while lounging around in the sun with a cold après beverage, such as a Skid Spritz or a Corpse Reviver. You can prep all the toppings beforehand and keep them in a cooler to pull out when ready. The pizza dough recipe makes enough for three ten-inch pizzas. Make the dough ahead of time and pull it out of the freezer the morning of. But if you're feeling lazy, your favorite store-bought ball of pizza dough will also do the trick.

---

**Makes three 10-inch pizzas**

### FOR THE PIZZA DOUGH

3 ½ cups all-purpose flour, plus more as needed

1 packet (¼ ounce) active dry yeast

1 teaspoon kosher salt

1 teaspoon sugar

1½ cups cold water

2 tablespoons extra-virgin olive oil

### DIAVOLA

1 pizza dough

½ cup tomato sauce

1 teaspoon kosher salt

To make the dough, mix the flour, yeast, salt, and sugar in a stand mixer on low speed with the paddle attachment. With the mixer on low, slowly add the water.

Switch to the dough-hook attachment and run on low speed for 8 to 10 minutes, until the mixture is no longer sticking to the bowl. If it sticks, add flour 1 tablespoon at a time. If it's too dry, add a small amount of water.

Remove the dough, split it into three pieces, and place them on a baking sheet. Drizzle with the olive oil and cover the sheet with plastic wrap. Let sit for 2 to 3 hours or individually bag and freeze immediately.

To make the pizza, preheat your pizza oven to max temp.

*Continues on next page*

5 ounces mozzarella, sliced

2 ounces thinly sliced spicy salami

4 pickled mini italian peppers

1 sprig fresh basil, chopped

Hot sauce, for serving

## BASIL, CORN, AND HONEY

1 pizza dough

½ cup ricotta cheese

1 teaspoon kosher salt

Kernels from 1 ear of corn

1 sprig fresh basil, chopped

Honey, for drizzling

## MUSHROOM PESTO

1 pizza dough

½ cup Everyday Pesto

1 teaspoon kosher salt

5 ounces mozzarella, sliced

8 to 10 mushrooms, sliced

¼ red onion, thinly sliced

Sprinkle flour or cornmeal on a pizza peel.

Stretch the dough into a thin 10-inch circle on your pizza peel.

Spread the sauce, ricotta, or pesto evenly across the dough and sprinkle with salt.

Layer the remaining ingredients on top of the sauce in the order listed (if you're using fresh basil or honey, reserve it for after cooking).

Turn your pizza oven down to medium temp, then slide the pizza into the oven in one motion.

Cook for 1 minute, rotate the pizza, and cook for an additional minute until the cheese is melted.

Remove from the oven and slice and serve immediately.

**SKID HACK:** When time doesn't allow for homemade pies, take a tip from our friend Shane Robinson: Create three sandwiches from one purchased pizza by stacking two slices together, topping to topping, and wrap each in foil. These make great quick snacks over the course of a longer day!

# THE SKID PIZZA

So your friends decided to have a pizza party at the trailhead, but you didn't get the memo? Don't show up empty handed! Stop by the frozen aisle of the closest grocery store (or gas station) and pick up a frozen pie to toss in the oven. Spruce it up with a few fresh ingredients, and nobody who's been traversing snow all day will know the difference.

**Makes 1 pizza**

1 (10-inch) frozen pizza of your choice

½ green bell pepper, thinly sliced

½ fresh tomato, thinly sliced

Pinch of cornmeal

1 sprig fresh basil, chopped

Be nice. Ask your friends if you can use their preheated pizza oven.

Sprinkle the cornmeal on a pizza peel.

Make sure to unwrap your frozen pizza before placing it on the pizza peel.

Top with the fresh bell pepper and tomato.

Turn the pizza oven down to medium, then slide the pizza into the oven in one motion.

Cook for 5 to 6 minutes, rotate the pizza, and cook for an additional 3 to 4 minutes, until the cheese is melted and the dough is cooked through.

Remove from the oven, sprinkle with basil, and serve immediately.

# BAIL CAKE

Not every day in the mountains goes as planned. And if it did, it probably wouldn't be nearly as alluring to seek out big lines on our skis. We prepare as much as we can, but sometimes the stars don't align, and we're forced to tuck tail and retreat from our objective. To reward ourselves for listening to the mountains and practicing patience, we started the tradition of Bail Cake. It's exactly what it sounds like: a cake we eat when we bail from our initial plan or objective. It's an easy one-bowl cake (since big objectives often leave us starved for sleep) made with ingredients we often already have on hand and a variety of easy-to-substitute berries, citrus, and sweeteners. Minimal prep, maximum reward. It's a sweet reminder that the mountains will always be there.

**Makes one 9-inch round or 8-inch square cake**

1 cup plain, full-fat yogurt

½ cup coconut sugar

¼ cup maple syrup

3 eggs

1 teaspoon vanilla extract

Zest from one orange or lemon

⅔ cup all-purpose flour or a gluten-free all-purpose flour mix

½ cup spelt flour (or substitute with all-purpose, whole wheat, or gluten-free mix)

½ cup almond meal

1 ½ teaspoons baking powder

½ teaspoon kosher salt

1 cup berries of your choice (we like a mix of raspberries and blueberries), divided

2 teaspoons white sugar, for topping

Powdered sugar, for dusting

Ice cream, for serving

Preheat the oven to 350 degrees F and butter or grease an 8-by-8-inch square baking dish or a 9-inch, round cake pan.

In a medium bowl, stir together the yogurt, coconut sugar, and maple syrup.

Whisk in the eggs, then add the vanilla and citrus zest (the more the better!).

Add in the flours, almond meal, baking powder, and salt. Stir well.

Carefully fold in the berries (trying not to mush them) and reserve a handful to sprinkle on top. Raspberries are the most delicate (and also the most delicious).

Sprinkle with the white sugar and bake for 32 to 38 minutes, or until a knife in the center comes out clean. Add a dusting of powdered sugar and 1 scoop of ice cream for each hour before 6:00 a.m. that you got up today.

Enjoy on the couch with your feet up.

**SKID HACK:** Make two of these cakes and freeze them for the ultimate lazy dessert when you arrive home totally wrecked from a hard day.

TAILGATE TREATS 209

# EAT PASTA, SKI FASTA

Our friend Kyra Foley likes to make this meal the night before a big day of climbing or skiing. Kyra calls it "the perfect creamy mushroom and lemon pasta dish; it's warm, cozy, and filling without leaving me bellyache bed-ridden for the night. Now, this is the recipe I gravitate toward when I know I am going to be waking up early and pushing my body." It also works well as a post-adventure meal. To make this vegetarian, skip the sausage or replace it with veggie sausage.

## Makes 4 servings

1 pound pasta, such as fettuccine or spaghetti

2 tablespoons unsalted butter

4 cloves of garlic, finely chopped

1 shallot, chopped

Pinch of kosher salt

Pinch of ground black pepper

1 tablespoon red pepper flakes

8-ounce variety pack of fresh mushrooms, thickly sliced

¼ cup heavy cream or crème fraîche

Handful of parsley, chopped

2 lemons, juiced

8 ounces spicy italian sausage (optional)

½ cup grated parmesan

1 cup microgreens (optional)

Boil a large pot of water for the pasta. Heavily salt the water and follow the cooking instructions on the box of pasta.

While the pasta is cooking, heat a large pan over medium heat and add the butter.

Sauté the garlic and shallot for 3 minutes, until softened. Season with salt, black pepper, and red pepper flakes.

Add the mushrooms and stir to coat with the butter.

Once the mushrooms start to soften (after 2 to 3 minutes), add the heavy cream or crème fraîche and continue stirring while it comes to a simmer.

Turn the mushroom sauce to low heat and add the chopped parsley and juice of 2 lemons.

In a separate cast iron pan, brown the sausage over medium-high heat and break it into crumbles. Cook for 6 to 8 minutes or until cooked through.

When the pasta is cooked, drain it, reserving ½ cup of the starchy pasta water. Add the pasta and reserved water directly to the mushroom sauce. Stir to coat the pasta with the mushrooms and sauce.

Serve the pasta topped with sausage crumbles, parmesan cheese, and a handful of local microgreens.

# ACKNOWLEDGMENTS

This collection of ski snacks is a love letter to the Tetons, our community of friends and family, and a celebration of enjoying good food in the mountains.

We want to thank Ariel Kazunas, Kaylee Pickett, Jack Beighle, Sarah Duggan, Katie Lozancich, Madison Ostergren, Kyra Foley, Nicole Jorgensen, Taylor Fry, Zach Montes, John Plack, Shane Robinson, Shelby Smith, Nora Fierman, Nicole Jorgensen, Katie Matthews, Kyra Foley, Helen Lewis, and Matt Dillon for their culinary expertise, nutritional advice, and inspirational contributions to this book.

Thank you to our friends in the Tetons Zac Montes, Maggie Shipley, James Temple, Molly Belk, Charlotte Percle, Nick Braun, Laura Gaylord, Josh Braun, Kailey Mckenna, and Pete Stone, for being the ultimate dinner party club. Sharing meals with friends in the mountains is better than any powder day we could dream up.

Thank you to Sophie Fearon for supporting our books and spreading the Beyond Skid love in Colorado, as well as all the other small businesses and bookshops that have supported the brand.

Finally, we want to thank our families Cynthia, John, and Henry Krass, and Erika and Gerd Ritter for the lifetime of inspiration in and outside the kitchen.

And thank you to anyone we've ever shared a chairlift, summit snack, or powder day with. This book wouldn't exist without you.

*Opposite: Cooking dinner on an overnight ski tour in the Tetons*

# RECIPES BY RATINGS

## ● GREEN

Aioli, Three Ways, 59

Ants on a Date, 84

Apple-Brie Prosciutto Roll-Ups, 97

Bacon-Wrapped Dates with
   Goat Cheese, 89

Bribery Banana Bread, 154

Chocolate-Blueberry
   Recovery Smoothie, 196

Chocolate Chairlift Cookies, 162

Classic Caprese, 126

Iced Earl Grey Maple Tea, 183

The Italian, 185

Le Chamoniard Baguette, 117

Miso Honey-Lemon Water, 173

Miso Peanut Sauce, 65

Oatmeal Banana Cookies,
   Three Ways, 80

Pesto, Egg, and Avocado, 112

Pocket Dillas, Four Ways, 138

Quick Candied Spiced
   Nuts, Four Ways, 105

Salted Maple Iced Coffee, 192

Salted Maple Lemonade, 193

The Skid Pizza, 207

The Spaghett or the
   Skid Spritz, 189

The Tram Waffle, 130

Tomato Jam and Arugula
   Breakfast Sammie, 114

Turkey, Apple, Brie, and Honey, 129

## ◼ BLUE

Bacon and Date Rice Bars, 76

Bail Cake, 208

Berry Chia Yogurt Parfait, 199

The Brooklyn Italian, 141

Butter Mochi Cake, 168

Charcuterie Board, 203

Cheesy Polenta Bars, 78

Chocolate-Dipped Pocket Bacon, 90

Chunky Monkey Smoothie, 187

The Corpse Reviver, 191

Crispy Nut Butter Bars, 92

Dirty Honey Chai Tea, 179

Eat Pasta, Ski Fasta, 210

Energy Balls, Five Ways, 72

Everyday Pesto, 61

Fudgy Espresso Brownies, 146

Homemade Nutella, 68

Jammy Banana Thumbprints, 82

Kimchi Grilled Cheese, 134

Lemon Yogurt Cake, 144

Mads Balls, 94

214 SKI SNACKS

Mini Orange Marzipan Cakes, 160
Mudslide Mocha, 177
The Older but Not Grown-Up
　　Old Fashioned, 190
Powder Day Turkey Club, 123
Quick Plum Rhubarb Jam, 67
Scallion and Cheese Waffles, 164
Smashed Chickpea and Avocado, 120
Sundried Tomato and
　　Olive Tapenade, 62
Trail Mix Chocolate Chip
　　Cookies, 150

◆ **BLACK**

Backcountry Biscuits, 166
Cinnamon Roll Flatbread, 152
Grilled Halloumi and Harissa, 124
Handheld Apfelstrudel, 157
Miso Ramen Broth, 181
Onigiri, Three Ways, 98
Pocket Quiche, Two Ways, 86
Schnitzel Strips, 108
Skid Luxury French Toast PB&J, 132
Soul-Warming Carrot
　　Ginger Soup, 174
SPAM Musubi, 103
Tailgate Pizza, Three Ways, 205

# INDEX

## A

Aioli, Three Ways 59
alcoholic beverages
    Corpse Reviver 191
    Older But Not Grown-Up Old Fashioned 190
almond butter 30
alpine picnics 52
Alps 19, 52, 157
altitude, cooking at 54-55
aluminum foil 41
Ants on a Date 84-85
Apfelstrudel, Handheld 49, 157-158
apples
    Apple-Brie Prosciutto Roll-ups 97
    Handheld Apfelstrudel 49, 157-158
    Turkey, Apple, Brie, and Honey Sandwich 129
arugula 114-115, 125, 129, 139, 141
avocado
    Pesto, Egg, and Avocado Sandwich 112-113
    Smashed Chickpea and Avocado Sandwich 120-121

## B

backcountry biscuits 166-167
bacon. *See also* meat
    Bacon and Date Rice Bars 28, 41, 76-77
    Bacon-Wrapped Dates with Goat Cheese 89
    Chocolate-Dipped Pocket Bacon 42, 90-91
    stocking of 31
baguettes 30, 117, 136-137
Bail Cake 208-209
baked goods
    backcountry biscuits 166-167

Bribery Banana Bread 154-155
Butter Mochi Cake 168-169
Cinnamon Roll Flatbread 152-153
description of 143
Fudgy Espresso Brownies 37, 146-147
Handheld Apfelstrudel 49, 157-158
Lemon Yogurt Cake 41, 49, 144-145
Mini Orange Marzipan Cakes 33, 160-161
Trail Mix Chocolate Chip Cookies 30, 42, 150-151
baking sheets 37
bananas
    Bribery Banana Bread 154-155
    Jammy Banana Thumbprints 82-83
    Oatmeal Banana Cookies, Three Ways 80-81
bars
    Bacon and Date Rice Bars 28, 41, 76-77
    Cheesy Polenta Bars 78-79
    Crispy Nut Butter Bars 92-93
Basil, Corn, and Honey pizza 206
BBQ Beef Onigiri 100
Bean and Cheese Dilla 139
beeswax wrap 42
Berry Chia Yogurt Parfait 199
Berry Chocolate Chip Cookies 80
beverages. *See* sippables
blender 37
bonking 25, 46
bread 118-119
breakfast
    Pesto, Egg, and Avocado Sandwich 112-113
    Tomato Jam and Arugula Breakfast Sammie 114-115
Bribery Banana Bread 154-155

brie
  Apple-Brie Prosciutto Roll-ups 97
  Turkey, Apple, Brie, and Honey Sandwich
    129
Brooklyn Italian 141
brownies 37, 146-149
burritos 47
butter 29
Butter Mochi Cake 37

## C
cakes
  Bail Cake 208-209
  Butter Mochi Cake 168-169
  Lemon Yogurt Cake 41, 49, 144-145
  Mini Orange Marzipan Cakes 33, 160-161
candy 28-29
canned goods 30
Carrot Ginger Soup 174-175
Carrot Zucchini Pecan Cookies 81
cashew butter 30
chai tea 179-180
Charcuterie Board 203
cheese
  Apple-Brie Prosciutto Roll-ups 97
  Bacon-Wrapped Dates with Goat Cheese 89
  Cheesy Polenta Bars 27, 78-79
  description of 31
  Halloumi and Harissa Sandwich 28, 49,
    124-125
  Turkey, Apple, Brie, and Honey Sandwich
    129
chickpeas 120-121
chocolate
  Chocolate Chairlift Cookies 42, 162-163
  Chocolate Chip Cookie Dough Energy Balls
    73
  Chocolate-Blueberry Recovery Smoothie
    196-197
  Chocolate-Dipped Bacon Bites 20
  Chocolate-Dipped Pocket Bacon 42, 90-91
  Crispy Nut Butter Bars 93
  description of 30

Trail Mix Chocolate Chip Cookies 30, 42,
  150-151
Chunky Monkey Smoothie 187
cinnamon
  Cinnamon Apple Date Cookies 81
  Cinnamon Roll Flatbread 152-153
  Cinnamon Sugar Almonds 105
Classic Caprese 126-127
Classic Tuna Mayo Onigiri 99-100
coconut milk 30
coconut oil 29
coffee 185, 192
condiments 32
cookies
  Berry Chocolate Chip 80
  Carrot Zucchini Pecan 81
  Chocolate Chairlift Cookies 42, 162-163
  Cinnamon Apple Date 81
  Jammy Banana Thumbprints 82-83
  Oatmeal Banana Cookies, Three Ways 80-81
  Trail Mix Chocolate Chip Cookies 30, 42,
    150-151
cooking at altitude 54-55
Corpse Reviver 191
Crispy Nut Butter Bars 92-93

## D
dates
  Ants on a Date 84-85
  Bacon and Date Rice Bars 28, 41, 76-77
  Bacon-Wrapped Dates with Goat Cheese 89
Diavola pizza 205-206
Dirty Honey Chai Tea 179-180
Double-Shot Mocha Energy Balls 72
dried fruits 30
drinks. *See* sippables

## E
Eat Pasta, Ski Fasta 210-211
eggs
  Pesto, Egg, and Avocado Sandwich 112-113
  stocking of 31
Energy Balls, Five Ways 37, 43, 72-73
equipment 34-35, 37

espresso 185
Everyday Pesto 37, 61

**F**

flake salt 29
flatbread 152-153
flour 30, 33
food processor 37
French toast 132-133
fruits 30. *See also* specific fruit
Fudgy Espresso Brownies 37, 146-147

**G**

goodie bag 43
gourmet snacker 44-45
grains 29-30
grilled cheese 134-135

**H**

Halloumi and Harissa Sandwich 49, 124-125
Handheld Apfelstrudel 49, 157-158
hard-sided plastic containers 43
Homemade Nutella 68-69, 130, 152
honey
    Honey Pistachio Energy Balls 73
    Honey-Lemon Water 49, 173
    Turkey, Apple, Brie, and Honey Sandwich 129
hunger 38-39
hydration 38, 79, 171

**I**

iced coffee 192
Iced Earl Grey Maple Tea 183
Italian Dilla 139

**J**

jam
    Jammy Banana Thumbprints 82-83
    Quick Plum Rhubarb Jam 67
    Tomato Jam and Arugula Breakfast Sammie 114-115
    Jammy Banana Thumbprints 82-83
jarred goods 30-31

**K**

Kimchi Grilled Cheese 43, 134-135
knife 35
kosher salt 29
Kyrgyzstan 127

**L**

lab rat snacker 44-45
Le Chamoniard Baguette 42, 117
Lemon Yogurt Cake 41, 49, 144-145

**M**

Mads Balls 94-95
Maldon Sea Salt Flakes 29
maple syrup
    description of 34-35
    Salted Maple Iced Coffee 192
    Salted Maple Lemonade 193
marzipan 32
measuring cups 35
meat. *See also* bacon
    BBQ Beef Onigiri 100
    Powder Day Turkey Club 49, 123
    Schnitzel Strips 27, 108-109
    stocking of 31
    Sweet Chicken Dilla 139
mega snack 47
milk 30
Mini Orange Marzipan Cakes 33, 160-161
miso
    Miso Honey-Lemon Water 49, 173
    Miso Peanut Sauce 65
    Miso Veggie Onigiri 99-100
mixing bowls 35
Mochiko flour 32
mooch snacker 44-45
Mudslide Mocha 177
Mushroom Pesto pizza 206
musubi 103

**N**

Norwegian waffles 131
nut(s)
    description of 30

Homemade Nutella 68-69, 130, 152
Quick Candied Spiced Nuts, Four Ways 105-106
nut butters
Crispy Nut Butter Bars 92-93
description of 30
Nutella, Homemade 68-69, 130, 152

## O

Oatmeal Banana Cookies, Three Ways 80-81
oils 29
Older But Not Grown-Up Old Fashioned 190
Onigiri, Three Ways 98-100
Ortler mountain 19
oven thermometer 37

## P

packaged snacks 28-29
packaging
aluminum foil 41
beeswax wrap 42
hard-sided plastic containers 43
resealable plastic bags 37, 42
silicone bags 42
takeout containers 43
pans 37
pantry 29-33
parchment paper 37
parfaits 199
pasta 210-211
peanut butter 30, 65, 132-133
Peanut Butter Coconut Energy Balls 73
personal motivations 26-27
pesto
Everyday Pesto 37, 61
Mushroom Pesto pizza 206
Pesto, Egg, and Avocado Sandwich 112-113
picnics 52, 196
Pico de Orizaba 16
pizza
Skid Pizza 207
Tailgate Pizza, Three Ways 205-206
plastic bags, resealable 37, 42
plastic containers, hard-sided 43

Pocket Dillas, Four Ways 41, 138-139
Pocket Onigiri 49
polenta 27, 78-79
pots 37
Powder Day Turkey Club 49, 123
puff pastry 30

## Q

quesadillas 138-139
quiche
Pocket Quiche, Two Ways 86-87
Quiche Épinard 86-87
Quiche Lorraine 87
quick bites
Ants on a Date 84-85
Apple-Brie Prosciutto Roll-ups 97
Bacon and Date Rice Bars 28, 41, 76-77
Cheesy Polenta Bars 27, 78-79
Chocolate-Dipped Pocket Bacon 90-91
Crispy Nut Butter Bars 92-93
description of 71
Energy Balls, Five Ways 37, 43, 72-73
Jammy Banana Thumbprints 82-83
Mads Balls 94-95
Oatmeal Banana Cookies, Three Ways 80-81
Onigiri, Three Ways 98-100
Pocket Quiche, Two Ways 86-87
Schnitzel Strips 27, 108-109
SPAM Musubi 103
Quick Candied Spiced Nuts, Four Ways 42, 105-106
Quick Plum Rhubarb Jam 67

## R

ramen 181-182
recipe ratings 50
resealable plastic bags 37, 42
rolled oats 30

## S

salt 29
Salted Cocoa Pecans 106
Salted Maple Iced Coffee 192
Salted Maple Lemonade 193
sauces and spreads

INDEX 219

Aioli, Three Ways 59
description of 57
Everyday Pesto 61
Homemade Nutella 68-69, 130, 152
Miso Peanut Sauce 65
Quick Plum Rhubarb Jam 67
Sundried Tomato and Olive Tapenade 62-63
Scallion and Cheese Waffles 164-165
Schnitzel Strips 27, 108-109
science food 25
seeds 30
silicone bags 42
sippables
Chunky Monkey Sippables 187
Corpse Reviver 191
description of 171
Dirty Honey Chai Tea 179-180
Iced Earl Grey Maple Tea 183
Italian 183
Miso Honey-Lemon Water 49, 173
Miso Ramen Broth 181-182
Mudslide Mocha 177
Older But Not Grown-Up Old Fashioned 190
Salted Maple Iced Coffee 192
Salted Maple Lemonade 192
Spaghett 189
skid 10, 13
Skid Crepe 139
Skid Luxury French Toast PB&J 132-133
Skid Pizza 207
Skid Spritz 189
Smashed Chickpea and Avocado Sandwich 120-121
snacking frequency 46
snacks
amount of 46, 63
flowchart for selecting 44
making your own 25-29
packaged 28-29
personal motivations for 26-27
routine for 28
timing your eating of 38
variety of 46

Snickerdoodle Energy Balls 73
soup 49, 174-175
Spaghett 189
SPAM Musubi 103
spices and seasonings 29-30
summit sandwiches
Brooklyn Italian 141
building of 118-119
Classic Caprese 126-127
description of 111
Halloumi and Harissa Sandwich 28, 49, 124-125
Kimchi Grilled Cheese 43, 134-135
Le Chamoniard Baguette 42, 117
Pesto, Egg, and Avocado Sandwich 112-113
Pocket Dillas, Four Ways 41, 138-139
Powder Day Turkey Club 49, 123
Skid Luxury French Toast PB&J 132-133
Smashed Chickpea and Avocado Sandwich 120-121
Tram Waffle 130-131
Sundried Tomato and Olive Tapenade 62-63
survivalist 44-45
Sweet and Spicy Walnuts 105
Sweet Chicken Dilla 139
sweeteners 30, 34
syrup, maple 34-35

### T

tailgate treats
Bail Cake 208-209
Berry Chia Yogurt Parfait 199
Charcuterie Board 203
Chocolate-Blueberry Recovery Smoothie 196-197
description of 195
Eat Pasta, Ski Fasta 210-211
Tailgate Pizza, Three Ways 205-206
tailgating 196
takeout containers 43
tapenade 62-63
tea
Dirty Honey Chai Tea 179-180
Iced Earl Grey Maple Tea 183

220 INDEX

thermometer 37

thermos 37, 178

toaster 37

Tomato Jam and Arugula Breakfast Sammie 114-115

tools 34-35, 37

Trail Mix Chocolate Chip Cookies 30, 42, 150-151

Tram Waffle 130-131

trial and error 16, 19-20

turkey
Powder Day Turkey Club 49, 123
Turkey, Apple, Brie, and Honey Sandwich 129

Turmeric Ginger Cashews 106

## U

under-eating 63

## V

vanilla 169

vegetables 30

## W

waffles
description of 30
Scallion and Cheese Waffles 164-165
Tram Waffle 130-131

water 38

# ABOUT THE AUTHORS

Max and Lily met on a backcountry yurt trip in the Front Range of Colorado. After attending the University of Colorado—Boulder, they moved to the Tetons. Depending on the season, you'll find them skiing in Grand Teton National Park, ripping singletrack on Teton Pass, or whipping up a new creation in the kitchen of their tiny apartment.

In addition to their all-consuming addiction to powder skiing (which does take up almost forty hours a week), Lily is the editor of *The Ski Journal* and a ski guide for Exum Mountain Guides, in the winter, and Max is the gear editor at *Powder Magazine* and a freelance writer and photographer.

Learn more about them and check out their first cookbook *Beyond Skid: A Cookbook for Ski Bums* at their website, www.beyondskid.com.

*(Photo by Zach Montes)*

## ABOUT SKIPSTONE

Skipstone is an imprint of independent, nonprofit publisher Mountaineers Books. It features thematically related titles that promote a deeper connection to our natural world through sustainable practice and backyard activism. Our readers live smart, play well, and typically engage with the community around them. Skipstone guides explore healthy lifestyles and how an outdoor life relates to the well-being of our planet, as well as of our own neighborhoods. Sustainable foods and gardens; healthful living; realistic and doable conservation at home; modern aspirations for community—Skipstone tries to address such topics in ways that emphasize active living, local and grassroots practices, and a small footprint.

Our hope is that Skipstone books will inspire you to effect change without losing your sense of humor, to celebrate the freedom and generosity of a life outdoors, and to move forward with gentle leaps or breathtaking bounds.

All of our publications, as part of our 501(c)(3) nonprofit program, are made possible through the generosity of donors and through sales of 700 titles on outdoor recreation, sustainable lifestyle, and conservation. To donate, purchase books, or learn more, visit us online:

www.skipstonebooks.org
www.mountaineersbooks.org

SKIPSTONE
LIVE LIFE
MAKE RIPPLES

## YOU MAY ALSO LIKE

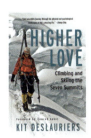
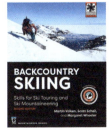
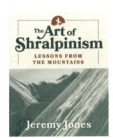